Permission to Be

Permission to Be

ERIC BLAKEBROUGH

daybreak
London

First published in 1992 by
Daybreak
Darton, Longman and Todd Ltd
89 Lillie Road, London SW6 1UD

ISBN 0–232–51962–5

A catalogue record for this book
is available from the British Library

Cover: Sarah John

Phototypeset by Intype, London
Printed and bound in Great Britain
at the University Press, Cambridge

Contents

Acknowledgements

After Mary, my closest companion, I am indebted to the members of the John Bunyan Baptist Church, Kingston-upon-Thames, who have given me the privilege of being their minister for 25 years. It has been an exciting time, far more productive than any of us could have imagined. Thanks be to God.

I am grateful to Adele, my associate minister, and to my friend Ian Hargreaves for reading the manuscript and for his comments and suggestions. I particularly thank Sue Rich, my personal assistant, who has typed the manuscript and made many helpful comments as we have written the text. And finally, my thanks to Morag Reeve for encouraging me to write this book and my publishers, Darton, Longman and Todd, who have completed the task.

Preface

This book is about church worship, personal prayer and social action. It used to be thought necessary to strike some kind of balance between the spiritual and social aspects of Christian faith. It is now generally recognized that the two belong together. Even so, many are searching for an appropriate spirituality which holds together both our experience of God and our participation in society. This calls for a reassessment of traditional Christian worship and prayer in the light of modern living conditions.

The book clearly reflects my own experience, but the pattern of spirituality which is described has developed over a period of more than two decades within a Christian congregation, the members of the John Bunyan Baptist Church, Kingston-upon-Thames.

As a congregation in a London suburb where the drug scene flourished in the 1960s and continues unabated to this day, we became aware of the problems of many of the outcasts of our society. We became convinced that the gospel applies to society as well as to individuals and that the central message of Jesus is the kingdom of God. We formed the Kaleidoscope Project specifically to bring our neighbourhood closer to our understanding of the kingdom of God. This entailed providing residential, social and medical facilities for approaching 300 drug users who attend our centre daily; all this with a view to creating a more compassionate environment in which people might live more fully.

The kingdom of God (the phrase could be translated 'rule of God') needs to be understood in personal and social terms. This means realizing God's permission for us to be more fully ourselves by his indwelling and to be active in achieving a society which is more in conformity with God's will.

The book is structured in three parts to consider respectively church worship, personal prayer and the Christian's role in society.

Many Catholics, Charismatics and Anglicans have written books on spirituality in recent years, but there are also many in the Reformed tradition who are searching for a new direction. In some respects this search for a new lead requires us to understand better the traditions we have received from the past so that we can cut back to our roots in order that new growth might take place.

Eric Blakebrough
January 1992

1

Permission to Be

We are going through a transition in spiritual matters. The Victorian era had a pattern of spirituality known to a majority of English Protestant Christians. That pattern has been lost to most evangelical Christians in the last decades of the twentieth century.

Because Christianity is rooted in the historic revelation of God in Jesus Christ, it is assumed by many that beliefs and practices must remain unchanged. This explains some of the opposition within the Roman Catholic and Anglican Churches to changes in liturgy; and it partly explains why many evangelical Christians have given such an unreserved welcome to styles of worship which recall features recorded in the Book of Acts. There is an obligation upon Christians to remain faithful to Jesus and the Apostles; but an equal obligation exists to make a coherent presentation of the gospel which takes account of new knowledge and new conditions of life.

It would be eccentric to fit a Victorian kitchen into a modern house. The pace of life, for one thing, does not allow the laborious processes familiar to Victorian cooks. Patterns of spirituality must similarly adjust to the conditions of modern living. Christian lifestyles which were familiar to many believers in the early decades of the twentieth century no longer serve well the present generation of Christians.

Let me therefore describe a pattern of spirituality I inherited partly from my parents and partly from the evangelical circles I joined in my late teens.

The week began with Sunday worship. There were three services: 11am until 12.30, Sunday school from 3–4pm and the evening service beginning at 6.30 and usually finished by 8pm. The morning service was for the instruction of believers while the evening service was meant to bring unbelievers to faith in Jesus Christ. The sermon in the evening service often followed a familiar pattern although considerable ingenuity was exercised by the preacher to base his message on a different passage of Scripture. The basic message was: we have all sinned; we all deserve to suffer damnation; Christ died on the cross bearing our punishment; we can have forgiveness of sins and eternal life simply by asking God to accept us for Christ's sake. The message was powerful because it reached our sense of guilt, it explained what was wrong with the world and it showed us a way of salvation. At its deepest level it assured us of God's love.

We sang: 'Amazing grace, how sweet the sound that saved a wretch like me' and 'Blessed assurance, Jesus is mine'.

Midweek, there was the Bible study and prayer meeting. Here we became familiar with God's pattern of salvation from the dawn of creation right through to the second coming of Christ and the end of the world. These truths were not taught as myths, but as veritable facts more certain indeed than scientific theories.

We were taught that we should spend a period in personal devotions every morning and evening. For at least twenty minutes, we read a dozen or so verses of the Bible with the help of 'Bible Reading Notes' followed by personal prayers. We were taught that these prayers might profitably follow a pattern of thanksgiving and praise, confession of sins and intercessions.

There were certain characteristics of a Christian lifestyle. We avoided swearing and sexual jokes. We tried to 'set an example' at school or at work. We believed it was 'unspiritual' to go to the cinema, to dance, to sing popular songs, to gamble or to drink alcohol.

Relationships with the opposite sex were strictly controlled. Boys were told that it was natural to be attracted to girls but that the attraction was so great that it was undesirable to get too close. Girls were told it was their Christian duty not to dress or behave in any way which might inflame improper desires in boys. We were assured that sex was good provided it was approached with caution and avoided if possible: somewhat like a high explosive!

In evangelical circles, it was customary for a father to conduct family prayers in the home. This consisted of a reading from the Bible followed by short prayers. Grace was said before meals, and even in restaurants we usually bowed our heads in prayer momentarily before eating.

These practices gave us a sense of identity as Christians. With this sense of identity came the comfort of knowing God was present with us in all the circumstances of our lives. It meant that we were constantly in contact with God.

When I went into the Royal Air Force as a youth of seventeen and a half, I went as a Christian. I knelt by my bed in the billet morning and night and this act of commitment made me a witness for Jesus Christ

3

throughout my time in the forces. I met other evangelical Christians and we became a Gospel Witness Team.

These personal recollections will be familiar to millions of evangelical Christians worldwide, but most people today are unfamiliar with this religious lifestyle.

There are many reasons why these features of my early Christian life no longer fit my present lifestyle. My former routine was based upon a regular daily and weekly time-table. I was an instructor in the RAF which meant that I worked from 8am until 4pm every weekday and went home every weekend, except on the rare occasions when I was required for guard duty. My pattern of work over the past 23 years since my appointment as minister of the John Bunyan Baptist Church in Kingston-upon-Thames, and since becoming Director of the Kaleidoscope Youth and Community Project, has been quite irregular. Until recently, I worked all night Fridays in the Kaleidoscope club. On Saturdays I prepare my sermon for Sunday. Sermon preparation is a form of prayer in which one tries to be open to the inspiration of God. This reading, thinking, writing and meditating process may occupy three hours at a stretch. My mind continues to work on my sermon through Saturday's sleep and I wake Sunday morning to work again at copying out the headings of my sermon. I then go to the church where I conduct Sunday morning service. I suppose I pray very little on Fridays, but on Saturdays and Sundays I am in some kind of prayerful state for about eight hours out of the 24 hours I am awake.

On Mondays, I am usually exhausted. On Tuesdays, I wake early and start to prepare for the Kaleidoscope staff meeting, seeking inspiration for my leadership of the team. On Tuesdays, Wednesdays and Thursdays, I

4

celebrate Holy Communion at 9.30am and usually work through the day until late evening. On Fridays I make a late start to the day but continue with only meal breaks right through till midnight or into the early hours of Saturday. I used to work in the Kaleidoscope club from 10pm on Fridays until 6am on Saturdays, but I can no longer sustain this duty.

In such a busy schedule, regular times for personal prayer are not possible. It is clearly not a satisfactory way of living. For this reason, staff at Kaleidoscope have four-day breaks every three weeks.

On these regular days off, I go to Wales where I drink in the beauty of that land and my spirit rejoices in God. When I am in Wales on a Sunday, I usually attend the Roman Catholic Mass, one reason being that the preaching service in the Baptist chapel is in Welsh which I do not yet understand.

Even allowing for four-day breaks, my life is too crowded. The same is true for most of my church members, many of whom leave home before 8am and do not return until 7pm. They hardly have time for breakfast and hurry their evening meal if they are to get to choir practice, the church members' meeting, or other engagements. When do they find time for courting, or family life? When is there time for recreation? Favourite television programmes, a disco or a concert, a meal at a restaurant or participation in sport: these all result in a late night. My church members share the same pace of life common to most busy people in this modern age.

The compensation for this pressure of modern living is longer holidays and more frequent bank holidays. Compared with former generations who often went without holidays, or only had one or two weeks a year, many of us enjoy more than one annual holiday and up to nine days of bank holiday. Incidentally, this irregular pattern of our working lives plays havoc with traditional church life based on a weekly programme. Members are no longer present every Sunday, nor can leaders be found for many midweek activities.

This new pattern of alternating periods of intensive work activity and free leisure time gives many of us opportunities of participating in residential retreats or events such as Spring Harvest. My own church arranges retreats at bank holidays, running from Fridays to Mondays, at Pencilmaren, our retreat house in Wales.

I have attempted to show some of the changes which may occur in the pattern of spirituality being adopted by an increasing number of Christians. People often feel anxious about any such changes. We all cling to rituals of one kind or another and we are uncomfortable with changes in these routines. It is helpful to recall that Jesus and his disciples found it necessary to break away from some of the traditional practices of the orthodox Jews of their day. Jesus apparently kept the main religious festivals but he and his disciples did not feel bound to observe all the fasts practised by religious people in their day (Matt. 9:14). The disciples were not anxious about the distance they travelled on the Sabbath or about grinding corn in their hands as they walked together (Matt. 12:1–8). Jesus taught that slavish obedience to traditions and rituals was not what faith was all about.

The important truth to grasp is that we do not have to follow any particular pattern of personal devotions. A single person working nine to five with not much travelling might find morning and evening prayer times most satisfactory. But a couple with a new-born baby demanding feeding every four hours will almost certainly not find a regular pattern of prayer possible.

Do not be anxious. God is not over-demanding. Learn to love God spontaneously.

Perhaps it is audacious to apply the words of Frank Sinatra to our spiritual experience, but his phrase, 'I did it my way', hints at the freedom we should apply to our relationship with God.

PART I

In Church

2

Homeless Christians

Many Christians no longer feel at home in their own churches. Not only has there been a sea change in the pattern of daily life, there have been great shifts in church life also. Churches in which people were brought up and in which they received their faith have in many cases changed beyond recognition.

In many churches the furniture has been moved. The position of the altar has changed, or more likely, the old altar has been left where it was and a new, less substantial one, has been placed rather awkwardly in front. In some cases, a collection of band instruments stands untidily at the front where the choir used to sit and the ubiquitous overhead projector sits precariously on its small stand opposite the white pull-down blind which is its screen. The worshippers no longer bring their familiar leather-bound Bibles and service books with them, but are faced in the pew with a bewildering selection of multi-coloured paperback song books and duplicated sheets of paper.

These things are disturbing enough in the house of prayer, but it is what these things signify which is the real problem. Many church communities have changed theologically. For instance, were my old theological college Principal, Dr Arthur Dakin, to revisit this mortal scene

11

and enter any one of several Baptist churches he knew well in former times he would presume it was no longer a Baptist church but a Pentecostal one. If the venerable doctor witnessed what went on in one of the house meetings and heard talk of First, Second and Third Waves (Pentecostal movement, Charismatic movement and Charismatic renewal respectively) he would assume he was at a gathering of some new religious sect.

Well, why should there not be radical changes in churches if everything else is changing? Indeed, anything which is living must change and theology, being the intellectual and spiritual discipline of making sense of how we think about God in the light of new knowledge and new situations, must change also. There are discernible changes even in the churches described in the New Testament within decades of the day of Pentecost.

Change there must be. A Christian has no right to expect a church to be cosy. Theology has moved on since the days of Dr Dakin. The ecumenical movement has been responsible for some liturgical changes. Society has changed and this in turn changes the prevailing mood.

Theology has changed partly as a result of biblical studies. In the USA there is strong pressure from some quarters to resist any fresh interpretation of the Bible, and American Baptists are now split into two movements; the one accepting an interpretation of Scripture which would commend itself to most universities in Europe, the other fundamentalist movement rejecting any serious modification of traditional views. Bible scholars propose new interpretations as a result of new knowledge and on-going debate. The results of such biblical criticism take a long time to filter through to local churches but gradually a change of emphasis takes place. Whereas a preacher previously might appeal to the authority of the Bible by simply quoting a proof text and saying, 'the Bible says', the preacher today is more likely to refer to experience as proof of the truth of the Christian message. A policeman told of how he was converted under the ministry of Cliff Richard. The policeman said that Cliff Richard simply gave the challenge, 'Try it for yourself; if you find the Christian faith works for you, fine, if not, leave it'. The policeman committed his life to Jesus and found that the gospel worked for him.

John Macquarrie, the Oxford theologian, has detected a similar movement in theological studies. In his book, *Paths in Spirituality*, he has devoted a chapter to 'Subjectivity and objectivity in theology and worship'. He traces a movement going back as far as Schleiermacher but in modern times starting with Karl Barth and following through Rudolf Bultmann and Dietrich Bonhoeffer to the present day; a movement towards subjectivism. Macquarrie comments:

> In the theology of our time, then, subjectivism is on the up-swing. Perhaps it was necessary that there should be a move in this direction, and it probably has helped to make faith more lively and personal for many people.

Macquarrie goes on to say:

> But when subjectivism reaches its extreme pitch and the objective elements in Christian faith are abandoned altogether, then, as I see it, the duty of the sane theologian is to hold the line and to stress the objective elements in Christian faith in the face of the subjectivizing flood.

Sociology would confirm that the present age is one which looks for spontaneous experience. Perhaps it has something to do with 'science-fatigue', a feeling of rebellion against the idea that everything is fixed by factors which can be objectively discovered and manipulated only by experts. The rest of us want some part of the action.

For these reasons, and no doubt there are many more, the Charismatic movement has gathered pace in many churches. Instead of instruction in the Christian faith, those who want to know God are urged to seek a deeper intuitive knowledge coming through the Holy Spirit. The term 'baptism of the Holy Spirit' is understood as a release of God's power into the lives of those who open themselves to the Spirit. The outward manifestations of this indwelling are the gifts of the Spirit described in 1 Corinthians 12, and in particular speaking in tongues and prophecy are seen as indicative of this spiritual breakthrough.

This experiential approach to Christianity has proved dynamic to a great many people who previously found nothing to interest them in the Church. Many church members who had felt a lack of spiritual power in a declining church have found new life as a result of this dependence upon the Holy Spirit. The Charismatic movement is the fastest growing part of the Church today.

It may be accepted that the Charismatic movement is of God. But there is a danger that those who are involved in this renewal believe that it is the one-and-only movement of God today. As a matter of fact, it is not. There are varieties of gifts as St Paul reminds us in 1 Corinthians 12, and in Chapter 13 he points to the superiority of love over other gifts and to his preference for coherent statements of faith (theology and preaching) over ecstasy.

Those of us who do not wish to speak in tongues nor join in some of the singing ask that our gifts are also recognized and used.

There have been many periods in church history when something akin to Charismatic renewal has taken place. There is never an unaltered repeat performance, but the present Church scene is not entirely new. Fashions come and go in church as well as in the street. How many evangelicals remember singing Sankey's *Sacred Songs and Solos* and CSSM choruses? They were good days, singing our heads off to the accompaniment of the harmonium in the back hall of the chapel, but it won't do today.

Faith needs firm foundations. We must know Christ first and foremost, we must know the Word of God in the Bible (which is not the same as knowing the text) and we must know the presence of the living Lord Jesus through the work of the Holy Spirit in the sacraments and in our worship. We need to emphasize these essentials and not give anything else the same priority.

In these days of theological and spiritual ferment it is inevitable that there will be some movement from one local church to another and even from one denomination to another. In the present confused situation we must be prepared to support both those who stay in churches where they no longer feel at home but remain to bear witness to their faith, and those who feel called to move out and join new fellowships.

The wider community

Apart from these internal matters, many Christians are concerned about the relationship between the Churches and the wider community. There was a time when most people in Britain had at least a nominal allegiance to a church. Perhaps it was only a link through the Sunday school, a uniformed youth organization, a women's meeting or some form of social activity. The Baptist church I attended before going to theological college had a membership of less than 100 but there were in those days 300 children on the Sunday school roll and our Boys' and Girls' Brigades could put on a good parade led by a competent band. On monthly parade Sundays the church would be full, on Sunday school anniversaries there would be standing room only. Easter was not such a popular festival in the Free Churches but candlelit carol services at Christmas were a very popular innovation. Moreover, when you went door-to-door visiting most people welcomed a caller from the church even though they felt a little embarrassed as they explained why they did not regularly attend.

Not only was there local goodwill, you felt that politicians listened to the voice of the Churches. Today, if the Archbishops of both the Anglican and Roman Catholic Churches make a statement it will be reported and some kind of response will be made. But the voice of the Free Churches is rarely heard.

This lack of influence is disappointing but only a symptom of something much deeper. The Churches have largely lost credibility with the public and no longer play a significant role in civil life. The symbols are still there: the Mayor has a Chaplain, prayers are said in Parliament and in the local Council meeting, the Judges process to church accompanied by civic dignitaries; but it is ancient custom rather than an expression of the nation's faith.

Church members who are involved in politics are particularly aware of the withdrawal of the Church from the public sector. Even among non-governmental organizations the Churches are now only rarely represented.

It may be the case that the Church has lost the intellectual high ground, but there is not much evidence of this. It is more likely that the Church, which has continued through missionary societies and aid organizations to make a major contribution to the life of other nations, has lost confidence in its ability to contribute to the further development of our own society. Yet it is at this time above all that we need to hear the voice of prophets — not on the domestic scale giving guidance as to the whereabouts of some missing asses (1 Sam. 9:20) but on matters of national importance.

It is never easy to discern the Word of God for a nation at a particular time. Wealth creation and increased efficiency are clearly in line with the biblical ideal of good stewardship. It is inevitable that some people will make greater effort than others and it seems fair that their work should be rewarded.

It has been shown that under the Communist system a lack of sufficient individual incentive and too much regulation of production and distribution results in low efficiency, a denial of personal freedom and a poor standard of living for the population as a whole.

Even modest regulation of market forces proves difficult to achieve. An Incomes Policy proved unacceptable to Trades Unions, and so-called Independent Review Bodies cannot really be independent of government if salaries are to be paid out of taxation.

Public expenditure even on such priority areas as health, education, housing and pensions can only be allowed to grow as a nation prospers. If industry is to remain competitive in world markets, advanced technology with less

17

labour seems inevitable with consequent high levels of unemployment.

Given the complexities of the problems, it cannot be expected that the preacher has the answers. The slogan 'Jesus is the answer' is absurd. Which is why so many Church leaders refrain from making political statements and many church-goers prefer it this way. When the Church at an Assembly or through some other official body makes a critical comment, politicians demand that it stops interfering in politics and concentrates on spiritual matters.

Evangelical churches in particular call upon individuals to repent of their sins and accept Jesus Christ as their personal Saviour and Lord. The evangelist proclaims the universality of sin and the salvation which Christ obtained when he died once and for all on Calvary. In a sense, this message stands outside of time and does not relate to particular issues of the day, which is why many people who take life seriously tend not to take the Church seriously.

An understanding of the whole gospel requires Christians to become more attentive to political matters in order to discharge their duty as agents of the kingdom of God. This will involve a hard discipline of reading, thinking, discussion and action. This is what it means to consecrate oneself to the fulfilment of God's purposes for the world. Politics is distasteful to people who like their religion to be transcendental, immortal, invisible and unrealistic. But for those inspired by Jesus' proclamation of the kingdom of God, the task must be undertaken to bring society closer to that ideal.

The Christian preacher, no more than the Hebrew prophets of old, cannot be expected to prepare Bills for

Parliament, but he or she must question the morality of political decisions. Some inequality in life is inevitable, but it cannot be right for the majority of people to enjoy increasing prosperity at the expense of a significant proportion of the population who are experiencing increasing hardship. The dramatic reduction and redistribution of employment in manufacturing industries in recent years has created areas of high, long-term unemployment resulting in human misery. Meanwhile the arrangement of taxation in the same period has favoured the rich and disadvantaged the poor. In the post-war period up to the mid-1970s the divide between rich and poor narrowed and the quality of life for all sections of the community improved. Since then, the gap has been increasing and there has been growing inequality in income, housing, education, public services and civic amenities.

Total spending on Social Security has gone up, partly due to an increase in the number of pensioners, but largely because of the steep rise in unemployment. Time and again the Government has chosen to present the facts in ways which suggest that the unemployed and those on State benefits are apathetic, unenterprising and prone to scrounging. They are not regarded as typical British citizens. They are not seen as the victims of changed circumstances. At this time of real hardship for those at the bottom end (including more families with children than pensioners), those at the top of the income scale are enjoying substantial tax benefits. This increasing gap between the poor and the rich is dividing our nation with evil consequences. The Archbishop of Canterbury has spoken of the link between violence and social deprivation. Such violence is indeed a manifestation of wickedness, but the blame must be properly apportioned to include the

Government. People will endure hardship provided the cause is perceived to be just, but the young will act in anger against society if it appears that the system is unfair.

Unemployment, homelessness and the increasing divide between the rich and the poor are moral issues. Government policies must change to bring about greater social justice in these areas of our national life. Church bodies have not the expertise to propose the ways and means to achieve these ends but the Church must point to where changes need to be made. As unemployment is likely to continue rising in the foreseeable future, a more adequate income must be paid to the long-term unemployed. Homelessness must be reduced and targets must again be set for house building. The Government should bring forward proposals for improving the lot of those living below what might generally be regarded as a reasonable quality of life in our society. Health, education and the economy will continue to dominate public debate, but issues such as racism, world development and ecology require greater public awareness. In all these matters, the Church must become better informed and increasingly active.

The need for compassion

The quality we most need to recover in our nation's life is compassion. Compassion is quoted most frequently in the New Testament as the driving force and main characteristic of the ministry of Jesus. Compassion is closely related to that other New Testament term 'grace'.

To begin with a bit of background. There has been a reaction in both the nation and the Church in recent years against what was perceived to be the permissiveness of the 1960s. A reassessment of doctrine by some theologians led to a new understanding of morality. The belief in 'absolute moral standards' was brought into question. Paul Tillich wrote, 'Love alone can transform itself according to the concrete demands of every individual and social situation without losing its eternity and dignity and unconditional validity' (*The Protestant Era*, p. 173).

Naturally, the Pope reacted against this 'new morality', pointing out that this love ethic could be used to justify a Catholic leaving the Roman Church if it seemed to bring him closer to God, or it could justify the use of contraceptives if that seemed to enhance personal relationships!

This debate on morality has divided the Church in recent years and dismayed many politicians who feel it is time to recall the nation to the 'old values'. The renewed emphasis upon law and order is part of this reaction.

Clearly, relationships need to be based upon integrity and mutual respect. Yet ethics are bound to reflect people's collective experience and be expressed in working definitions of what is 'right' and 'wrong'. In this way relationships become codified by means of law. But law has the capacity to condemn rather than to restore people who are conscious of failure.

I work with drug dependents. These people are all criminals in that they use illicit drugs. Their habit can cost between £50 and £100 a day and as most of them are unfit for work which might provide a sufficient level of income, most are involved in further criminal activity. In order to provide food and clothing for themselves and their children they are tempted to engage in shop-lifting. Many of these people are homeless or housed in the worst conditions. But their greatest burden is their sense of worthlessness. Prostitution for some of them is the outward expression of their inward feelings of degeneracy. They use foul language and are violent because that is what they feel is appropriate for their condition. Some are employed and many have high standards, but they know they are walking near the gutter.

The public demand police action to rid the community of such people. They are frequently arrested and they represent a large proportion of our prison population. Some are victims of AIDS and are likely to spread the disease to others.

The law is powerless to help. All attempts to remedy the situation by means of law enforcement have repeatedly failed. Treatment and rehabilitation programmes are in the main designed to help those who are motivated to come off drugs, but efforts to care for those who feel that abstinence is unrealistic for them are not well supported.

There is a way, a long-term approach, which offers hope to people such as those I have described. It is the way of compassion. In practice this means providing social facilities such as a club and a coffee bar, it means providing medication to reduce the need for illicit drugs and help modify mood swings. A free supply of condoms, needles and syringes helps prevent the spread of AIDS. But above all, it needs an understanding of people who feel themselves to be aliens in their own community and estranged from themselves and their families.

This is a specific example of the failure of a system of law and the practical outworking of a Christian understanding of grace. What I see in the area of my own work, I am sure applies more generally. The unemployed, the poor, the inadequate, the under-achievers, the homeless and families struggling to live on Social Security have all been made to feel in a large measure to blame for their misfortune. These people need to feel welcomed back into the care of the community. This is not simply a matter of improved social benefits, although these are important, it is a deeper understanding of their situation and a recognition that we all belong to one another which is most needed.

The Christian Church should be the source of this much needed compassion. This will only happen if we rediscover the New Testament teaching on law and grace. What St Paul and Luther discovered before him, John Bunyan discovered for himself in his study of the Bible and in the light of his own experience. Puritan preachers saw two opposing systems at work, or 'Covenants' to use their term. There is a Covenant of Law and a Covenant of Grace.

Bunyan understood the Covenant of Law in a particular way in the circumstances of his day. Personally he felt convicted of being a serious sinner. He was troubled that he had transgressed God's law and that he was unacceptable to God. He knew that if being clear with God meant being free from sin, he was not in the clear. If God dealt with people on the basis of law, Bunyan was condemned to hell.

Bunyan saw that the clergy, the landlords and the magistrates of his day were, if anything, in a worse state before God. The civil and ecclesiastical authorities were an unholy alliance as in the time of Christ. They upheld this Covenant of Law because it protected their privileges and kept the poor in conditions of misery. They were the worst kind of hypocrites and would go down to hell.

But Bunyan came to know God on an alternative basis, the Covenant of Grace. He entitled his spiritual autobiography, *Grace Abounding to the Chief of Sinners*. It might seem an exaggeration to call himself the chief of sinners but he says in his autobiography: 'I did still let loose the reins of my lust, and delighted in all transgressions. I was the very ringleader in all manner of vice and ungodliness.'

Bunyan discovered two sets of texts in Scripture. According to one set of texts he was condemned because he had broken God's laws, but according to other texts God was willing to receive and forgive sinners. After a prolonged period of spiritual conflict, Bunyan trusted himself to the grace of God and found peace. He came to believe that for some reason of God's sovereign will all those who put their trust in him are accepted on the basis of God's Covenant of Grace.

There are some parallels between John Bunyan's times and ours. Christopher Hill, formerly Master of Balliol College, Oxford, writes of the despair of the poor in the late sixteenth and early seventeenth centuries. He suggests that anxiety was especially present because of the great economic divide in which the lucky few might prosper whilst the mass of their neighbours were plunged into deeper poverty.*

The situation is different in Britain today in that the majority of people in recent years have enjoyed increasing prosperity, but this makes it all the worse for the losers and those people living in areas of high unemployment who endure poverty. There is a great economic divide, and although poverty may not today be as bad in absolute terms, in relative terms (and these are the terms which matter) many people are experiencing poverty.

In these circumstances where we are likely to experience increasing social tension, governments will look to the

* See *A Turbulent, Seditious and Factious People*, p. 68.

Church to support tougher measures to strengthen law and order. Politicians will call upon the Church to condemn those who break the law. In this way the Church could be used as a buttress to help preserve the existing social order. The Church must resist being used in this way.

Jesus was put to death because the Scribes and Pharisees of the Law did not approve of his compassion for sinners. The Roman authorities acceded to the demand for Jesus to be crucified because of their concern for public order.

The Church cannot side with those in society who have power against those who are denied power. We acknowledge the necessity for just laws and we call upon people to obey the law, but unless there is a change of heart towards those who are being denied a reasonable quality of life, there will be no peace in our communities. The Church must preach the word of reconciliation because our gospel is not a gospel of law, but of grace.

It is profoundly discouraging to go to church and feel that the liturgy, the hymns and the sermon have nothing to do with life outside. I have sat in some chapels and almost seen the strange name Ichabod, meaning the glory of the Lord has departed (1 Sam. 4:21), written on the end wall. Simply changing the hymns and putting more energy into the service is not the answer. It is the content of the service that matters. The word of God most needed in today's society and the message most needful for people who know their sins is the gospel of grace.

3

Public Worship

Public worship is rarely entirely successful. Rabbi Lionel Blue confesses that 'for me the religious moments of my life, or the peaks, are usually on a park bench, in a pub, on a train'.* He says that he has periods in his life when public services of worship are very important but that at other times he gets nothing out at all.

A recurring theme in letters to the editor of the *Baptist Times* has been the strong feelings for and against modern trends in worship. This is not simply a matter of conservatism. Some of the most radical Christians dislike most of the latest popular worship songs, while many of those who hold most tenaciously to a conservative theology are enthusiastic followers of modern fashions in worship.

In some cases almost the entire congregation is united in their likes and dislikes, their theology and their life-styles, but in most congregations there is a measure of disagreement about such matters. Most families who attend worship regularly go home to Sunday lunch with some fairly robust comments about one or other aspect of the morning service. This can prove tiresome to younger members of the family who may conclude that there is so

* In Bax, Josephine, *Meeting God Today*, p. 43.

26

much dissension in the church that it seems pointless to get involved.

Public worship and different denominations

Anyone writing on the subject of public worship is bound to present one particular preference within the limitless range of valid patterns. Even within the main Christian denominations there are clear differences. The Orthodox Church which insists on a high degree of conformity tries to cope with differences of culture by conceding autonomy to the various ethnic groups within that communion. The Roman Catholic Church adheres to a universal structure but provides a choice of alternative liturgical prayers to give variety. The Anglican Church accepts a common prayer book with a series of alternatives. Even in these examples of congregations which emphasize a common tradition the local priest inevitably introduces significant innovations.

Among Nonconformist congregations there is apparent anarchy, but in truth, there is a remarkable degree of unity which defies rational explanation. There is a fundamental unity based upon an acknowledgement of Christ as Lord and Saviour, common Scriptures, the sacraments of baptism and the Lord's Supper, the Lord's Prayer and other common elements of liturgy and hymnology. Above all, there is a dependency upon the guidance and inspiration of the Holy Spirit.

Although Christians hold a great deal in common, it is inevitable when we attend public services of worship that we must submerge some of our personal preferences in the experience of the larger group of believers. This is bound to lead to some degree of irritation. We might sum this up in the Yorkshire saying, 'everybody's queer 'cept thee and me and even thou's a bit peculiar'.

What then is to be done about public worship?

Those churches which have a strong liturgical tradition believe that in outline their services preserve 'the shape' of worship going back to the apostolic period. It is reasonable therefore to ask people to accept a liturgy which has been carefully constructed by scholars who have studied documents relating to the early Church. Perhaps the standard work on this subject is *The Shape of the Liturgy* by Gregory Dix.

Protestant Christians begin with a deep suspicion of liturgical services presided over by a priest. The claim of the Roman Catholic Church that only their ordained priests have the power to forgive sins and to consecrate the bread and wine, to make present the body and blood of our Lord, is rejected. These 'powers' belong to the priesthood of all believers. This belief releases a congregation from dependence upon the ordained minister and gives the membership authority to determine what form public worship shall take.

Evangelical Christians of a previous generation inheriting this antagonism towards priests in the Catholic tradition thought they detected a similar conflict between priests and prophets in the Old Testament. Modern Old Testament scholars such as Gerhard von Rad believe that any such conflict has been greatly exaggerated. Free Church congregations nevertheless felt fully justified in rejecting liturgical forms of worship and concentrating on preaching the gospel backed-up with hymns and prayers. This led to the commonly accepted 'hymn-sandwich' type of service which was almost universal in Free Church congregations until recent years.

The modern Charismatic movement discerned that New Testament worship was Spirit-led. They rejected the monopoly of the ordained minister to lead every act of worship. Instead, they planned for a substantial period of celebration during which believers were free to engage in singing and public prayer. It was felt that many of the old hymns were dreary and over-burdened with doctrinal concepts. New songs were required which facilitated exuberant outbursts of praise and expressed more directly their spiritual experience. Charismatic churches feel justified in urging people to join in such celebratory worship because it represents a kind of worship suggested by some passages in the New Testament.

Orthodox, Catholic and Anglican churches are justified in giving a certain priority to the descriptions of worship which are recorded in documents going back to the first centuries of the Church. After all, we are dependent upon that generation of Christians who wrote down the New Testament and began the expansion of the Church from Jerusalem to the ends of the known world. Evangelicals are right to emphasize the importance of the gospel in every service of worship. Charismatics are right to assert that those who worship God must do so in dependence upon the Holy Spirit.

These three elements: apostolic teaching, the preaching of the gospel and the inspiration of the Holy Spirit must be held together. The precise way in which this is done will vary from time to time according to the various cultural and social conditions prevailing in any situation. Anyone studying for an examination in Religious Education will be familiar with the process of discovering the background to each book of the New Testament. Similarly, every group of Christians has a particular situation which affects to a considerable degree their understanding and experience of Christ. Patterns of worship vary accordingly. The study of liturgy shows that everything is possible and nothing is fixed.

Public worship and the local church

How then are we to settle upon an order of service for next Sunday's worship in our local church? In those churches with a hierarchy the problem has been solved already and the individual must accept a degree of discipline in this matter. Those denominations which give a large degree of autonomy to each congregation leave the members the daunting task of deciding the matter among themselves by a process of discussion, with prayer for the guidance of the Holy Spirit.

Allow me to describe the development of a pattern of worship in use at my own church, the John Bunyan Baptist Church in Kingston-upon-Thames.

Soon after my appointment as minister to the John Bunyan Baptist Church in 1967, dissatisfaction was expressed with the hymn-sandwich type of worship then in use. This dissatisfaction was particularly strong among a small group of young people who had recently left university and had come to our church to help in the development of our community work. There was not much complaint about my preaching I am glad to record but it was strongly felt that it was no longer acceptable for the entire service to focus upon the sermon, nor was it acceptable for the minister to lead the worship in a way which gave most of the members a largely passive role.

It is not entirely clear what prompted this dissatisfaction. It may have had something to do with the hippy movement with its emphasis upon spontaneity, and with the fact that some new members of the congregation had a Catholic background with an expectation of participation in a liturgy culminating in Holy Communion. It may have had something to do with modern education which encourages participation in a process of discovery rather than learning what teacher tells you.

The community work of my church through the Kaleidoscope Project brought us into contact with a great variety of religious tradition and experience. This compelled us to think seriously about an ecumenical commitment. We needed to find a pattern of public worship which would enable us to reach out towards the goal of visible unity for the whole Church. This visible unity cannot be restored unless each congregation becomes aware of the painful situation of our divisions and takes positive steps towards overcoming this disobedience to the will of Christ (John 17:1–26).

In deciding upon a framework for public worship, our church members deliberately adopted the division into two parts which is found in early liturgies of the Church and is a feature of modern Roman Catholic and Anglican worship. The first part concentrates on readings from Scripture and the sermon. The second part follows the description of the Lord's Supper in the New Testament.

The worship begins when a member of the congregation announces: 'We are here in the name of Jesus Christ.' The President responds: 'Jesus said, where two or three are gathered together in my name I am there among them.' There follows an act of confession with the absolution declared by the whole congregation. The Gloria concludes this opening section. The Scriptures of Old and New Testaments are read by members of the congregation. The minister, or other person appointed to do so, preaches the sermon. After the sermon a hymn is sung and then a member of the congregation leads us in prayer.

The second part of the service is well ordered but has a real sense of being directed by the Holy Spirit. The President, now standing at the table, exhorts us all: 'Lift up your hearts.' This is an instruction for all of us to 'be in the Spirit on the Lord's day' (Rev. 1:10).

We are reminded that our worship in time and space is linked to the eternal life of God. The congregation responds: 'We join in the eternal hymn of praise.' This communion with heaven is confirmed by the President's words: 'We join Mary, the Apostles, those who have gone before us in the faith, and all God's people saying: Holy, holy, holy Lord, God of power and might, heaven and earth are full of your glory, hosanna in the highest. Blessed is he who comes in the name of the Lord. Hosanna in the highest.'

The eucharistic prayer now follows. The President, who is usually the minister but may be a male or female member of the congregation specifically appointed to the task, now leads the eucharistic prayer. This prayer of thanksgiving includes the words of our Lord at the Last Supper and an invocation of the Holy Spirit that we may all discern the bread and wine to be for us the Body and Blood of Christ (1 Cor. 11:29).

The words used in the second part of the liturgy are important, but even more so are the actions. The four actions are clearly performed. Christ's action in taking the bread and cup is seen when children bring the bread and wine up to the table at the offertory. The action of Christ blessing the bread and wine is reproduced when the President stands with uplifted arms to give the eucharistic prayer. This prayer follows a traditional pattern but has spontaneous elements.

The final two actions of breaking the bread and giving the bread and wine to the congregation are done by the President and Deacons in almost total silence. There is a silence at this point which can be felt. It often happens that a baby who may have been crying earlier in the service instinctively becomes still at this moment.

There is nothing novel about this order of service. It is meant to reflect the earliest liturgies of the Church and to encompass the common heritage of the mainstream Christian Churches. There is considerable economy of words in the liturgical part of the service which enables us to sing three hymns and include a substantial sermon within the space of about an hour. We all know that there are congregations in other parts of the world who enjoy three-hour services, but this may have more to do with a different pace of life than with a deeper devotion to Christ.

Our form of service does not overcome the limitations inherent in every act of public worship, but it does provide six essential ingredients in the corporate life of every practising Christian:

1   It is an act of obedience to Christ where we try to submit our wills to his.
2   It provides an occasion for general thanksgiving and intercession.
3   It provides a focus of unity.
4   It enables the believer to 'receive Christ' as a continuous process of growth towards 'Christhood'.
5   It mobilizes the congregation for mission.
6   It enables the unbeliever to 'sample' the gospel.

1 *Obedience*

The root of sin is egocentricity. The virtue of Christ is his obedience to the will of God. Time and again the Gospels record that Jesus acted in obedience to God.

Put bluntly, Jesus commanded us to 'do' the Eucharist together regularly (on the first day of the week and often daily). This weekly assembly for the purpose of enacting the Eucharist was the definitive pattern of worship in the early Church. When Justin Martyr described Christian worship in about AD 150 he states:

> And on the day which is called the day of the sun, there is an assembly of all who live in the towns or in the country; and the memoirs of the Apostles or the writings of the prophets are read as long as time permits. Then the reader ceases, and the President speaks, admonishing us and exhorting us to imitate these excellent examples. Then we arise altogether and offer prayers; and, as we said before, when we have concluded our prayer, bread is brought, and wine and water, and the President in like manner offers up prayers and thanksgivings with all his might; and the people assent with amen; and there is a distribution and partaking by all of the eucharistic elements.

An examination of this description by Justin Martyr shows a close parallel to the order of worship at the John Bunyan Baptist Church which I have described.

There is scope for great variety of local tradition and practice. What is questionable is whether it has ever been proper for every group of believers to 'do their own thing' without any sense of obligation to do what Jesus and his Apostles instituted.

Worship must not simply be a matter of personal preference. Discipleship means being disciplined. Military metaphors are unfashionable but I know from my own service in the Royal Air Force that you cannot run a camp successfully without discipline. It is worth remembering that the word 'liturgy' originally referred to the duty rota of Roman soldiers. When an individual joins the church he or she must accept that they will be required 'to keep in step'.

The hippy movement which promised so much failed because its faith was too fragile and it rejected any concept of obedience. The Eel Pie Island Commune, which occupied a tiny island in the River Thames near Kingston-upon-Thames, was anarchical. Although there were some clearly visible leaders they professed belief in the total autonomy of each individual. After an initial euphoric period when some expressed pleasure in freely choosing to do the chores, all the unpleasant tasks were abandoned and the whole community life disintegrated.

The Kaleidoscope hostel is self-consciously anti-authoritarian where the only condition of residence is that a person does not attempt to destroy the community. Even so, it regularly becomes necessary for someone, usually staff, to call the residents together and provide leadership in cleaning the place up.

If people are to be disciples of the Lord Jesus Christ they must be obedient. Nonconformists reject hierarchical government, but they are wrong if they neglect a properly ordered weekly service of public worship based on the reading of Scripture, preaching and the breaking of bread.

2 *Thanksgiving and prayer*

One of the strengths of the Charismatic movement is that it has recalled the Church to thanksgiving and prayer. Eucharist means thanksgiving and this rightly implies celebration. Any service which is overburdened either by a sense of guilt or by an over-emphasis on social issues is discordant with the main theme of thanksgiving. Life is sustained on this planet to a very remarkable degree: let's give thanks!

3 *A focus of unity*

Individuals are not generally conscious of their need of solidarity with others. When companionship is obviously denied, a sense of loneliness is acutely felt. Also when an individual, a group or a nation feel a threat to their identity there is an immediate and urgent need of unity. People often turn to the Church when their national identity is threatened.

To the believer, the Church is his or her true family. To be cut off, or isolated from the Church is therefore a serious injury. There have been circumstances where to break away from the Church has been a matter of conscience, but otherwise loyalty to Jesus Christ demands solidarity in his Church.

A distinction has to be made between the need for the believer to be incorporated into the body of Christ which is the Church, and the obligation which a local congregation often tries to impose upon members. Many people quite justifiably feel that they cannot spare the time to be drawn in to the weekly programme of a local congregation. Where a person judges that they are fulfilling their

Christian vocation in their daily work and social life they will have to decide what proportion of time they can properly give to the programme of the local church. In some cases a believer should feel little obligation to become involved in anything more than participation in the Eucharist and whatever other commitments can realistically be undertaken.

I have noticed that some people who have been very active members of a local church, when they move away do not always take up membership in another. The reason is sometimes that a person no longer feels able to attend church once or twice on Sunday, help with the Sunday school or youth club, accept some office in the church such as secretary, treasurer or deacon, and be put under pressure to participate in house groups, working parties, prayer meetings, committee meetings *etcetera*.

Church members must be set free to work out their own vocation. A local church must resist the temptation to be too possessive of their members. More Christians need to work out their vocation in their work, in politics and in many of the organizations which contribute to the life of the community. Such commitments may prevent regular attendance at the local church's weekly meetings. Encouraging members to participate more in the life of the wider community would benefit both society and the church.

The sense of unity in the worship of the local church must not be too parochial. We need to feel oneness not only with the people in the pews next to us but a sense of unity with the whole Church of God. This is another reason why the local church in its public worship should have some regard for the pattern of worship in a majority of mainstream churches.

One of the most powerful means towards achieving the

visible unity of the Church would be a gradual converging of the different patterns of worship. This is not a plea for a uniformity of style. Sermons, songs and prayers will reflect the variety of Christian experience and the different ministries of local congregations.

In this matter of the visible unity of the Church, the role of the ordained ministry needs to be stressed. Non-conformists will certainly want to retain their freedom to appoint a layperson to preach and preside at the Eucharist in certain circumstances, but it should be seen as a temporary measure. Those who regularly lead a local congregation should be accredited representatives of the whole Church of God and should be suitably prepared, tested and ordained for this ministry. Such ordinations should include recognized church leaders and representatives of more than one congregation so that the ordained ministry represents the unity of the whole Church.

4 *Receiving Christ*

Each person has a unique contribution to make to the creative purpose of God. Even a stillborn baby created strong feelings within the mother and probably within a whole family. People are changed by such experiences. Each individual has their own special mutation to perform upon humankind. Such infinite variety is the glory of God's work of creation. Every person has God's special permission to be.

It is glorifying to God that individuals carry their own unique personality inherited and formed by the complex events of their own history.

The love of God sustains all life but there are occasions when people experience a form of 'imprisonment of the

38

spirit' when they no longer enjoy God's loving kindness. Public worship can be an occasion when a person finds liberation and a knowledge of God's sustaining love.

Of the many influences which make us what we are, we need education in the history of God's dealings with his people over all the generations of time and we need the inspiration of the Holy Spirit to draw us forward out of our mean-ness into the generosity and nobility of Jesus Christ.

In this process of growth towards 'Christhood' we need to be responsive to the words and acts of God, but above all we need to be receptive. Charles Wesley makes it plain that evangelical Christians truly believe in the real presence of Christ in the Eucharist:

> Our hearts we open wide
> To make the Saviour room;
> And lo! the Lamb, the crucified,
> The sinner's friend is come.

There must be stillness and silence in public worship to enable the believer to receive Christ. The life of God, eternal life or Holy Spirit, does not originate within us, worship must help us to receive the gift of God's presence.

5 Mobilization

A church is an agency of the kingdom of God in a locality. Just as Religious Orders concentrate on particular vocations (e.g. education, care of the sick or elderly, help to the poor) so it should be that every local church should be clear about their particular mission.

There are too many general-purpose churches with

all-purpose buildings. Such generalized ministries are often evidence that a congregation has not taken seriously their particular situation or opportunity.

A church, once in a fashionable residential district now become bed-sitter land for people on Social Security, needs radically to alter its whole programme. Mid-week talks are of little relevance. What is necessary is to convert the lower hall to a free launderette and enlarge the kitchen to provide cheap meals. Where the church used to provide accommodation to uniformed youth organizations they should now be planning a nursery open from 8am to 6pm for the use of single parents who need to work. In this situation the preacher had better avoid references to the sanctity of family life, bearing in mind that many people in the district are single. There would need to be no implied criticism of mothers who go out to work.

The particular ministry of a local church should not preoccupy the congregation but it should be clear what task has been entrusted to them by God. The call of God and the developing nature of its mission should be a regular theme in the preaching and intercessions of the local church. In this way, the Sunday worship should be an occasion when the entire congregation is mobilized for action. Unless a church exists for the sake of others it must be judged to be barren and allowed to die.

6 *Sampling the gospel*

Every service of public worship should be an occasion when an unbeliever can 'sample the gospel'. The sermon should always be capable of being understood by a person not used to theological language and biblical ideas.

Everyone needs to feel accepted by God and everyone of good will should go away with a sense of peace with God.

Everyone is welcome at the Lord's Supper as a visitor, but anyone attending regularly and wishing to take communion should discuss with the minister what it means to be in membership of that church. At some point it is appropriate for someone coming into membership of a local church to make a profession of faith and to be baptized if they have not previously received this sacrament.

These six considerations constitute an obligation upon all Christians to give a high priority to regular attendance at public worship. All believers are elected by God to be a corporate priesthood. Their sacred vocation is to offer up praise, thanksgiving, intercessions and service to God on behalf of the whole community.

4

Sermons

The emphasis of Protestantism has been on the importance of preaching, as opposed to the sacramental and
ceremonial elements in religion. At the time of the Refor-
mation many Protestants had a faith in the merits of sermons comparable to that which Catholics attributed to
the Mass. People would attend as many as three or four
preaching services on a Sunday. The middle class in towns
demanded preaching of a special kind, often with a political overtone. Where the parochial minister could not meet
this demand, a congregation might subscribe money to
maintain a lecturer for the purposes of preaching.

In Victorian times there were many famous preachers.
I have a photograph of the great Baptist preacher C. H.
Spurgeon, at the Metropolitan Tabernacle in 1891.
Spurgeon stands aloft in his central pulpit with row upon
row of faces looking towards him, the vast congregation
hanging on his every word.

C. H. Spurgeon preached at a time when the Free
Churches were at the height of their influence in Britain.
And the power of the Nonconformist movement was in
the preaching. Those preachers who drew overflowing
congregations had great oratorial powers and not all they
said was strictly confined to the biblical text. John Clifford

and Robert Hall before him were other great Nonconformist preachers who stirred the conscience of the nation
and dared to pronounce the Word of God on issues of
social justice and national politics.

It is unlikely that those days of large congregations gathering to listen to long sermons will return. Dr Billy
Graham, it is claimed, has preached to more people than
any previous living man but his campaigns are highly
organized and draw people from many congregations over
a wide area.

It is still customary in many Protestant churches to have
two preaching services on a Sunday. There was a saying
when I was a young man that the morning service was
for the 'saints' and that the evening service was for the
'sinners'. In those days you expected Bible exposition in
the morning and an evangelistic service in the evening.
But I wonder if the origin of the two services had more to
do with the class structure of Victorian society. An elderly
lady who died some years ago told me that when she was
'in service' as a young woman, the Master and Mistress
would attend the morning service and the servants were
required to attend the evening service. She added: 'The
people Upstairs were always very concerned about the
morals of the people Downstairs, but not so concerned
about their wages!'

Matthew Fox in his book, *Western Spirituality*, has suggested that the enthusiasm among Welsh Nonconformists
for preachers and preaching may have something to do
with Celtic culture. The Celts put great store on the bardic
tradition and honour the words of visionaries. This may
account for the fact that historically Nonconformist
preachers who have at their disposal all the rich imagery
of both Old and New Testaments, have captured the

imagination of Welsh people more readily than the aca-
demically trained Anglicans with their dry homilies, or
the even more foreign priests of the Latin Mass.

With these preliminary observations in mind we will
not want to elevate the sermon out of all proportion to
other elements in a service of Christian worship. We might
also wish to question the sacred tradition of two preaching
services on a Sunday. The recent trend in many churches
to bring together the sermon and the Holy Communion
and to give proper emphasis to both is most welcome.

Preaching needs to be about God. Because God is holy,
preaching about God will always be challenging. But God
is chiefly to be praised for his loving kindness and the
emphasis in preaching should be upon this nature of God
rather than the sinful nature of man. I only know a few
words of Hebrew but I remember from my days at theological college that a key word in the Old Testament is
chesed, meaning the loving kindness of God. This is to be
the dominant theme of preaching.

The Bible records the way in which God has been
revealed and the New Testament contains the witness of
the first generation of Christians to the life, teaching,
work, death and resurrection of Jesus. The Bible is therefore the basic text of the Christian faith. For this reason
preaching needs to be an exposition of Scripture. It is
highly beneficial if the minister of a congregation keeps
close to a lectionary so that the whole of Scripture and the
whole life cycle of Christ is imprinted upon the minds and
hearts of the congregation.

Preaching needs to be theological. That is to say, sermons should help us relate the historic faith of Christians
to our present day and our deepest needs. I recall one
embarrassing occasion when I heard a sermon given at a

service of induction for a new minister where the preacher used the letters of the minister's name to introduce the separate points of his sermon. I was sat next to the Lady Mayor and she turned to me and said, 'You are not a Baptist, are you?' I replied, 'Not this kind of Baptist!'

It is necessary for a preacher to be constantly reading theology. Those who regularly attend my church have, over a period of time, had a great deal of the substance of good theological books given to them. I do not mean that I quote chunks of theological writing, rather, I try to digest the writing until I can express it in my own words. I try not to over-estimate nor under-estimate my congregation. Fortunately it is no longer generally the case that the minister is better educated than the congregation, although some preachers appear not to have got over their theological college training and their sermons are too much like essays. Theology is an academic discipline, but a sermon is preached straight from the heart, not from a textbook.

There is a danger that the primary objective of preaching, which is to glorify God and help people to respond to him, is lost if the preacher focuses too minutely on the actual biblical text. Some congregations become Bible enthusiasts who expect the preacher, Sunday by Sunday, to give them new and fascinating information about the Bible. That can seem like real preaching, but in fact it encourages a love of the Bible which is not necessarily the same as a love of God.

If too sharp a focus upon the text of the Bible is the temptation for fundamentalists, too wide a focus upon world events and social issues is the temptation for radicals. It is essential to expound the Scriptures and to apply the gospel to present-day living but the overall purpose of the sermon is to reveal how God is present in our lives and to call us to repentance and trust in him. There will need to be some reflection upon events in the life of the congregation and to what is happening in the nation but services must not be overloaded with social and political issues. Christians should be enabled to 'discern the signs of the times', to see what is happening in the light of God's eternal purposes, but they are not coming to church to listen to the minister's opinions on current affairs. An interpretation of events which depends on a facile parallel with Scripture can be positively harmful.

The length of the sermon is of some concern. This is partly a matter of the style and skill of the preacher and the expectations of the congregation. Where a congregation has been brought up to appreciate and participate in a liturgical service which features the singing of well-known passages of Scripture, responsive prayers and meaningful ritual, the sermon is often short. In this case, people can give maximum concentration and if the preacher serves them well the brevity of the sermon is no disadvantage. On the other hand, in Free Churches where congregations expect longer sermons, there is the opportunity to gain the attention of people and to convince them of some aspect of the truth. There are advantages in sermons lasting more than a quarter of an hour providing they are cogent and reasonably eloquent.

Let us suppose the preacher has done his or her preparation conscientiously and well. The passage of Scripture has been read with the aid of good commentaries. The minister has reflected on the passage contained in the biblical text and related this to the present needs of the congregation. An outline or the full manuscript of the sermon is written out. The preacher must now consider whether the sermon as it stands will hold the attention and fire the imagination of the congregation. Perhaps some illustrations or examples are required, a touch of humour even. But most important of all: is this sermon the inspired Word of God for this congregation on this occasion?

This matter of inspiration is difficult to explain. It is not a question of oratory: do the words and images stir the hearts of people? The question is much deeper: is this sermon likely to help people know the presence of God with them in their need, or hear God calling them to accept a particular challenge, or to believe that God is ready and willing to accept, forgive, cleanse and bless them? I have on many occasions prepared a manuscript of my sermon in advance of Sunday and then spent half of Saturday night wrestling with the question: is this the Word of God for the people tomorrow? Often that test has proved negative and I have had to struggle in my mind until I have the assurance that having waited upon God I have received his Word. On many occasions this has called for a complete re-think of the sermon. This spiritual process is most demanding and heaven alone knows how many times I have fulfilled this responsibility.

Jesus in his earthly ministry challenged his hearers: 'If anyone has ears to hear, let him listen!' (Matt. 11:15). There were occasions when our Lord could not exercise his ministry among people because of their lack of faith. The congregation is no less responsible for the sermon than the preacher. Even a comedian or a musician will testify to the importance of an audience and recall particular places which traditionally have an appreciative audience. In the supremely important matter of us receiving Christ through the preaching of the Word it is of the utmost importance that everyone is waiting in expectation

47

and prayer. A preacher can actually feel if people are really waiting for the Word of God.

Neither sermons nor sacraments work automatically, both require the response of faith.

But what is to be done in those cases where the minister regularly fails to meet the spiritual needs of the congregation? This is a hard question because nobody can satisfy everybody's needs. Members of a church can help by making comments to the minister, provided this is done sincerely. It is most discouraging if a minister hardly ever gets any real feedback from a congregation. Preaching is in many respects a corporate activity and members of a church need to pray for this aspect of their church's ministry.

Too much dependence upon the preacher is a bad thing. There are plenty of well-informed Christians who regularly attend churches where the preaching is mediocre. There are many theological and spiritual books and not all are written for experts. A person who reads the Bible regularly and prayerfully will not want for spiritual nourishment even if he or she never again hears a sermon.

5

Baptism

I was about seven years of age when I heard of a scheme for earning pocket money. A local Anglican church was recruiting choir boys and there were significant sums of money to be earned from singing on Sundays and for weddings on Saturdays. I auditioned and was accepted. On about the third choir practice, the choir master asked how many of us wanted to go forward for Confirmation. I got the impression it went with the job so I indicated initial interest. The choir master then asked me to request my parents for my baptismal certificate because you could not be confirmed unless you had been baptized. I sensed then that there might be a problem but I went home to find out my baptismal status.

My father was very attentive to my enquiry and greatly surprised me by his answer. He said the choir master was in error and turned to passages in the Bible to show that baptism was not to be administered to infants, nor was the Church of England right to baptize without total immersion. I had no idea of my father's biblical expertise because although he had been brought up in the Christian Brethren he was at that period of his life not a practising Christian.

I returned to the choir master with a list of relevant

Scriptures to prove the error of the Church of England. The choir master was adamant, if I was unbaptized I could neither be confirmed nor continue as a member of the choir. I experienced discrimination against Nonconformists at an early age!

In my late teens, when I was converted in an interdenominational Mission Hall, I reconsidered my need of baptism. As the Mission Hall was not allowed under the terms of its constitution to administer baptism, I applied to a Baptist church which I had attended spasmodically as a child when I was sent to Sunday school.

My baptism was an act of obedience to the command of Jesus Christ and as a witness to my new found faith. I do not remember any reference to the Holy Spirit other than the baptismal formula: 'I baptize you in the name of the Father, the Son and the Holy Spirit.' I was then plunged under the water and came up again with a profound sense of joy.

Since then I have been a Baptist. There are other reasons for my being a Baptist, but my baptism by total immersion upon profession of faith in our Lord Jesus Christ was the beginning of my Church membership.

There seems to be little hope of reconciling the two practices of 'infant' and 'believer's' baptism. The difference in practice reflects in some degree a theological rivalry between those who stress the objective and those who stress the subjective aspects of the sacraments.

John Macquarrie in his book *Paths in Spirituality* has described it as a basic weakness of Protestantism that God's approach to man is thought of almost exclusively in terms of the word of preaching. He observes: 'The stress has always been on preaching, instruction, hearing, understanding, that is to say on what goes on in our minds.' Macquarrie describes this one-sided emphasis as a form of Docetism* because it denies the bodily nature of God's revelation of Jesus Christ. In the older Catholic tradition there is the recognition that man is an embodied creature. In this incarnational theology the purpose of the sacraments is seen as incorporation in Christ. This understanding of the sacraments fights against individualism and subjectivism.

It is obvious that the stress on infant baptism is almost totally objective, the baby being unaware of what is happening. In my baptism 'upon profession of faith in our Lord Jesus Christ' the emphasis was mainly subjective. There are dangers in either extreme position.

In Angola, in the capital city Luanda, there is a monument with pictures depicting the conversion of African slaves to Christianity. The Bishop is shown pouring water over slaves as they pass before him in chains. Soldiers of the Portuguese colonial army are in attendance to ensure that all are properly sprinkled and pronounced Christians in the name of the blessed Trinity. That ritual may have made an impression on pagan minds used to the practices of magic, but it cannot be identified with the life-changing sacrament described by St Paul in Romans 6.

What possible theological justification can there have been for that mass baptism carried out in the Portuguese colony? This is clearly a case where the objectivity of the sacraments had been over-stressed to the point of absurdity. The ritual had been separated from the preaching of the gospel and was void of faith in those who were being subjected to this indignity.

---

* Docetism: an early Christian heresy that the humanity of Christ, his sufferings and his death were apparent rather than real.

The problem today is that in some instances baptismal practice does not seem to be on a much higher level. Babies are brought to church by unbelievers and the child is thereafter given practically no further instruction in the Christian faith. One might say that in some such cases the sacrament has been aborted.

This is not the case in those instances where the child is brought to church by believing parents and is in reality incorporated into membership of Christ's body from the moment of birth. One Scripture has it that the child is sanctified by the very fact of being born of at least one believing parent (1 Cor. 7:14), but the clearest indication of the mind of Jesus is his command that children brought to him for blessing should not be refused (Mark 10:13–16).

In the case of a child of believing parents, those 'sponsoring' the child are relying on the objectivity of the sacrament: the child is saved by the gracious words and actions of Jesus. It is so because God wills it. In this case, it remains for the child upon reaching maturity to make his or her personal response of faith in the service of Confirmation.

Baptists will not easily concede that infant baptism is valid nor will they admit to any deficiencies in their services of believers' baptism by immersion. As one Baptist minister put it after a long discussion with the minister of another denomination: 'You continue to baptize in your way; we will continue to baptize in His!'

There is little doubt that the early Christians baptized converts to the faith by immersion, or at least by pouring a quantity of water over their heads. Pictures in the catacombs in Rome and the existence of early-fourth-century baptistries such as that found in the base of the leaning tower of Pisa, confirm that baptism in the New Testament was by immersion. Descriptions of the baptism of Jesus and of other baptisms recorded in the New Testament provide the pattern for total immersion. This mode of baptism brings out the meaning of the rite given by St Paul in Romans 6. The candidates are held under water for an instant to express their death to the old life of sin and their identification with the death of Jesus, and they are raised out of the water as a sign of their new life and of their sharing in the resurrection of Christ. This rite proclaims the gospel, involves the will and the emotions and evokes faith in the candidate and all who witness the event.

There are some occasions when the emphasis is too much upon the subjective experience of the believer. The candidate may give a testimony to his or her faith and even if there is no suspicion of exaggeration, it can leave a person who has been brought up in the Church since childhood with the dilemma: since I have experienced no such dramatic conversion I cannot see a sufficient reason to be baptized. There are many Christians who are held back from receiving the blessing of baptism because they cannot identify anything in their experience to justify this public act of witness. That is what is wrong when the subjective aspect of baptism is over-stressed. We need to emphasize the saving action of God in baptism rather than the faith of the candidate.

Because the membership of my church in Kingston-upon-Thames has been drawn from many traditions there is no single understanding of baptism. We all agree with baptism by immersion of those who are adult converts, but we are concerned for those who were baptized as infants and now feel that they have missed out on the spiritual experience of believers' baptism. We are not happy about rebaptizing people because this would seem to invalidate the faith of many of our members who were baptized as infants and later confirmed.

There needs to be a re-examination of baptismal practices in the light of ecumenical dialogues. This subject has been well explored in the World Council of Churches' publication *Ecumenical Perspectives on Baptism, Eucharist and Ministry*, edited by Max Thurian. The chapter on 'Convergence on baptism' is helpful and the chapter on 'Confirmation in the 1980s' contains the following observation:

> There is no reason that a rite of commitment could not sit comfortably alongside a renewed understanding of Christian initiation. Initiation into the body of Christ is by water and the Spirit. It is the rite by which one is endowered with all the privileges and responsibilities of the Christian community. It admits to the Supper. Later, at a time of religious maturity (completely independent of physical maturity or catechetical preparedness) those who so desired could make a public profession of their faith in Jesus Christ and a commitment to him. If they fell away and later returned to the Church, or if they entered a new plane of religious experience or growth and felt they wished to renew this commitment they could do so freely.

In accordance with this principle that those who enter upon a new plane of religious experience should be free to renew their commitment, we recognize three kinds of baptismal experience. Firstly, we practise baptism by total immersion of those who profess faith in our Lord Jesus Christ. This is our usual mode of baptism. Secondly, for those baptized as infants who feel a need for some reason to reaffirm their baptism, we invite them to come to the baptistry, to dip their hand in the water and make the sign of the cross. The use of water testifies that their infant baptism was in water and the sign of the cross testifies that their baptism was in the name of the Father, the Son and the Holy Spirit. This public act of witness testifies to their personal faith in Jesus Christ. Thirdly, we allow those who feel impelled by conscience to seek total immersion even though they have been baptized as infants to reaffirm their infant baptism in this way. It is made clear that this is a reaffirmation, not a rebaptism.

Christian conversion is for some people a Damascus Road kind of experience (Acts 9) and can be followed soon afterwards by the rite of Believers' Baptism. But there are others, baptized as infants but not regularly attending church, who come to Christian commitment at a later stage. These varieties of Christian experience give rise to the need for the once only sacrament of baptism to be reaffirmed when a significant turning point in a person's religious faith occurs.

Some people mature into Christian faith having come to church regularly since childhood. Their growth in grace may not have had any dramatic moments. Such people may not feel the need for the sacrament of baptism. The church will wish to explain the importance of public testimony to their faith in Christ, to encourage them to experience a strengthening of faith by the work of the Holy Spirit in the sacrament of baptism and to urge them to be like Christ in this way, but if this appeal does not make sense to a person we must not let them feel that their spiritual status is in question. A person who is coming to faith and Christian discipleship should always feel accepted in the Christian community. We are all learners and none of us has a right to God's mercy. We rely on the saving power of Jesus Christ, not on any merits of our own. No Church bye-laws can overturn the pronouncement of Jesus, 'All that the Father gives me will come to me, and anyone who comes to me I will never turn away' (John 6:37). In our enthusiasm for total immersion and the profession of faith in the person being baptized, Baptists are at risk of over-looking the supreme importance of the Holy Spirit in baptism. It is clear in the New Testament that baptism is the occasion when the Holy Spirit comes upon a person afresh. We must guard against referring to the Holy Spirit in impersonal terms as if this indwelling of God is some kind of substance or grace. Our relationship with God, like any other personal relationship, can vary in closeness. Baptism is the act of union with Christ and an occasion of great spiritual intensity. In order that the objective work of the Holy Spirit is realized it is customary to Lay Hands on the person being baptized with a prayer of invocation for the Holy Spirit.

Baptism is an initial event in the lifelong union between God and the believer. Baptism is what the Christian life is all about — dying to self, living to Christ (Rom. 6). Baptism is also the key to our understanding of our mortal death. In the Catholic funeral rite, as the coffin is brought into church, the priest reminds us that the deceased has already passed from death to life at their baptism. Baptism marks the transition from death to eternal life for the believer (John 11:25).

We must not draw too sharp a distinction between those who have no consciousness of God and those who have responded in faith to the gospel. As we are all made in the image of God we are all capable of responding to calls which go beyond our self-interest. Indeed, many people who do not profess religious faith are responsive to the Spirit of God.

All people have the same capacity for God. That is why all people search for some kind of meaning in their lives. In the case of unbelievers, they do not recognize any ultimate commitment but respond to life on an *ad hoc* basis. Many of their decisions will be in line with the will of God, but these decisions will not be made because of any prior commitment to God. The believer has come to recognize that a lack of commitment to God may have disastrous consequences for the individual and the whole world order. This recognition is referred to as the 'conviction of sin'. The decision to replace *ad hoc* obedience to the will of God by a real commitment of one's life is what is meant by 'conversion' (which may be a sudden and overwhelming change of heart, or it may be a gradual process). This change of heart, or 'repentance', is accompanied by an assurance of forgiveness and acceptance by God based on a knowledge of God's nature seen clearly in the life, deeds and teaching of Christ.

It may seem from the sequence of events that the initiative comes from the individual who makes his or her commitment to God, but further reflection will show that it was the Spirit of God which in the first instance was prompting our obedience. We also recognize that God in love has been waiting for our turning to him. This coming together of a person and God accomplished either at a moment of decision or over a period of time, results in spiritual regeneration. The person who previously lived in ignorance of God or in a state of indifference, now finds the true source and goal of their life. A fundamental change has taken place in the relationship of the person to God, the profundity of which can only be described in terms of the death and resurrection of Christ. The previous state is seen to be like that of those who in their ignorance or by their indifference acquiesced in the crucifixion of Jesus. That Jesus accepted the consequences of Man's sin and yet prayed for our forgiveness gives us the assurance that God accepts our repentance. The resurrection of Christ demonstrates God's power ultimately to overcome the evil consequences of our wrong decisions and wrong-doing.

Conversion is clearly not simply a matter of intellectual discovery but involves our wills and takes place even beyond the level of consciousness. What we decide in response to God is but a tiny matter in comparison to the immensity of God's love and power which now floods our being. This is the spiritual reality, the rebirth, to which baptism is inexorably linked.

It is impossible to programme the working of the Holy Spirit and for this reason it is unwise to legislate in the matter of baptism. We recall the words of Jesus: 'The wind blows where it wills; you hear the sound of it, but you do not know where it comes from or where it is going. So it is with everyone who is born from the Spirit' (John 3:8).

6

The Lord's Supper

The title, the Lord's Supper, reminds us that the sacrament at the heart of Christian worship was instituted by our Lord himself. The richness of meaning of this act of worship has given birth to a great variety of titles. It is called the Eucharist, or Thanksgiving; it is called the Mass which suggests a sacrifice; it is called the Holy Communion because it incorporates the worshipper into the body of Christ and furthers our development towards 'Christhood'. Perhaps the title most widely used is Eucharist.

There is no coherent view of the Eucharist in the New Testament. There is the instruction of Jesus that his disciples should 'do this' in remembrance of him and there are the words of institution in St Paul's first letter to the Corinthians 11:23–34. Otherwise there are passages which scholars describe as 'eucharistic' but these are interpreted in a variety of ways.

Clearly the question must be asked, what do we mean when we offer bread and wine, say a blessing, break the bread and then eat and drink together in obedience to our Lord's command? Even a superficial survey of the main interpretations given by the Church over the ages would require a large volume. We must be content with a glimpse at the main traditions and suggest how an ecumenically minded Christian might approach this act of worship.

There is much to commend the unadorned simplicity of the service of Holy Communion in the Free Church tradition. The words of institution are usually read, the bread and wine are placed on the communion table, prayers of thanksgiving are made, the bread is broken and the congregation eat and drink together. What could be simpler than that? The older form of the Latin Mass with various genuflections and ritualistic manipulations by the priest gave to non-catholics the appearance of a magical rite. Indeed, some popular notions about the Mass were clearly superstitious rather than Christian. Legends about the host (unleavened bread) bleeding after the prayer of consecration make it clear that many lay Catholics believed that the bread consecrated during Mass turned into flesh! I remember as a young evangelical asking a Catholic if the host tasted like meat. He assured me it didn't and referred obscurely to transubstantiation — a word neither of us understood.

There is no doubt that recent simplifications in the liturgy of the Mass and the use of English have made the service more accessible to Protestants. Catholic priests make it clear that no molecular change in the bread and the wine is implied by the words used in the eucharistic prayers.

Catholic and Protestant theologians in recent decades have tried to unwrap exactly what each tradition understands by the actions and words of the Eucharist. These theologians have reported substantial agreement. Of course, those Catholics and Protestants who have learnt to hate each other are unimpressed by the work of theologians, and in any case sectarian antagonism is largely based on non-theological factors

Those Catholic and Protestant Christians who have come together in discussion and ecumenical fellowship are impatient that Church leaders are over-cautious and reluctant to remove existing barriers to inter-communion. Indeed, many ignore the rules and take communion in each other's churches without fuss. In this and other matters it should be remembered that the Church discerns the guidance of the Holy Spirit not only by reference to theologians and Church leaders but by taking into account the 'gut feelings' of lay people also.

Through all the different traditions a basic pattern has persisted, and key words and actions are almost universal. It is also accepted that true worship must be made under the guidance and in the power of the Holy Spirit. St Paul in a postscript to the words of institution (1 Cor. 11:27–34) makes it clear that participants in the action are required to 'discern' the bread and wine in the Eucharist to be significantly different from bread and wine used at meal times.

Catholics and Protestants alike would agree that the bread and wine do not undergo any physical change but there are two significant differences between bread and wine at dinner, and bread and wine in the Eucharist: subjectively, we think of a meal simply in terms of bodily enjoyment and nourishment; we think of eucharistic bread and wine in terms of the body and blood of Christ offered up for our salvation. And objectively, the bread and the wine at meal time are provided as bodily food whereas the bread and wine of the Eucharist are given to us as a sign of the saving power of Christ being released within us. Both subjectively and objectively there is this tremendous difference.

If the word transubstantiation is a problem for us, we can go some way towards agreement with the idea of transignification. That things change their significance is easy to show. A ring on a first finger has a different significance to a ring on the fourth finger of the left hand in England, on the right hand on the Continent. Even so, bread and wine in a restaurant have a different significance to bread and wine consecrated in the words of the eucharistic prayer.

The word transignification does not, however, sufficiently emphasize that the bread and wine become a means of God's grace to us by the power of the Holy Spirit. True worship cannot take place without the action of the Holy Spirit. Without the work of the Holy Spirit there can be no Holy Communion. The Holy Spirit is God expressed in Jesus being created within us. In this regard it is proper to speak of the Eucharist as a miracle.

When we hear the words 'take this' in the Eucharist we recall that these are the words of Christ to us. What we are about to receive is not some-*thing*: we are receiving *Christ*!

Protestants are often offended by the claim that the Mass is a sacrifice. It is rightly affirmed that Christ died once for all on Calvary (Heb. 7:27). Catholics and Protestants agree on the uniqueness of Christ's sacrifice on Calvary. Jesus alone is the Lamb of God who takes away the sin of the world.

In the Mission Hall where I was converted, there was a blood-red banner stretched across the front of the gallery facing the congregation. In bold letters the banner proclaimed: 'We preach Christ crucified'. As I listened to the preaching of the Reverend William Barker, it was apparent to me that the crucifixion of Christ did not only take place in history: it is God's decisive overcoming of sin and death *now and forever*. The message was for me now! It was to all intents and purposes as if I was there at the crucifixion. Or, rather than making me to be a traveller in time and space, it is better to say that the crucifixion of Christ is an eternal event and therefore effective whenever a person responds to that awful and gracious action of God's dealing with sin.

Just as the preacher brings the death and resurrection of Christ alive to us as a contemporary event, so in the Eucharist the sacrifice of Christ becomes real for us at every celebration. The preacher in the Mission Hall and the priest in the Mass may not recognize each others orders, but truth to tell they perform a similar function: they both set forth the sacrifice of Christ for our salvation.

The more we think about the meaning of the Eucharist, the more it becomes apparent that we must at some point go beyond mortal thought. Understanding (theology) can only take us a small part of the way. Knowledge must be superseded by imagination; thought must give way to wonder. This transition is marked in many liturgies by the *Sursum Corda*: the exhortation, 'lift up your hearts'.

In John Bunyan Baptist Church, the President moves from the lectern where the Scriptures have been read and expounded to the table at the centre of the chapel. Then the President raises hands and looking round the congregation calls upon the worshippers: 'Lift up your hearts'.

We are being invited to look beyond the ordinary concerns of everyday life. We are to see our lives from the perspective of God's intentions for the world.

Let me give an example. Day by day I struggle with

my sense of vocation in working with drug dependents. People assume there is a sense of reward in knowing that some have found new life through the work of Kaleidoscope. Actually, there are few who are cured of their addiction. Mainly it is a case of caring for people for their own sake. I am constantly being made aware that the medical profession, the magistrates, the police, some Christians and the general public are not satisfied with this position. They ask me what success we have in changing people. It is only when I turn away from what people expect of me and contemplate the unconditional love of God that I am confirmed in my vocation to serve people as they are.

The aim of serving people for their own sake does not fit in with present notions of market forces, targets and getting results. Worship enables us to see things in a different light.

Jesus repeatedly contrasted public opinion with the will of God. The Beatitudes (Matt. 5:3–10) set forth a different value system to that existing in any present-day state. Again, following upon the Beatitudes Jesus makes many contrasts between what is generally considered right and his own understanding of God's will. In John's Gospel there are many instances where people fail to comprehend the truths Jesus spoke of.

The exhortation to lift up our hearts is the call in worship to see life as God sees it. A vivid example in Scripture is the Book of Revelation. John is a prisoner of conscience on the island of Patmos (Rev. 1:9). To the authorities and the general public John is a subversive of some kind. But John in worship on the Lord's Day (Rev. 1:10) was 'caught up by the Spirit'. He clearly saw things not visible to mortal eyes. World events and the tyranny which many people suffered during the latter period of the Roman empire were seen to be fully accounted for in the divine plan. John, as Jesus before him, understood his destiny to suffer and the ultimate vindication of his life. His worship gave him a hope where there was little naturally to hope for.

You need to get 'caught up in the Spirit' in worship, or you are simply not yet 'getting through'.

In worship one is trying to connect with God's will and God's life. Meditate upon the Psalms (forget the difficult bits for the present) or read Chapters 4 and 5 of Revelation. Again, do not get stuck with the details. Use your imagination to see God's throne above the world. Realize that because of the many terrible things happening in the world there is need of God's judgement (not punishment). Contemplate that there must ultimately be some authority declaring what is right and true. Bow down with the 24 'Privy Councillors' of heaven (Rev. 5:8 etc.) and give glory to God that Jesus, the Lamb of God, is worthy to declare God's overcoming of evil because he himself was executed by the evil intentions of society but has been vindicated by God.

The heightened sense of God's will being done in heaven sharpens our concern for his will being done on earth. That is why worship not only makes us aware of God's ultimate purposes, it makes us acutely aware of how we relate to each other. In the Lord's Prayer, the worshipper contemplates God's glory and his will being done eternally but immediately afterwards there comes the petition for forgiveness and the prayer for grace to forgive others. The contemplation of eternity sensitizes us to our life in society.

Once 'heaven is open' to us in worship we become

aware that man is not the measure of everything in the universe. The language of the Book of Revelation may not become natural to us, but we no longer believe only in the world of our five senses. Our communion with the risen Christ predisposes us to believe in the communion of saints. The familiar hymn rightly says:

> Yet she on earth hath union with
> God the Three in One,
> And mystic sweet communion with
> Those whose rest is won.

I recall a radically-minded Christian who had difficulty believing there was any life after death. She told me that she believed that once you are dead, that is the end. Several months later she told me that in giving herself to worship in the Eucharist it suddenly became clear to her that in God death is fully overcome. She did not try to explain this conviction. Some truths are grasped in worship which cannot be discovered by rational thought.

Those who have gone before us in the faith, like those in distant lands, are no longer readily accessible to us, but neither are they lost to us. We must not cling to them, be dependent upon them nor possessive of them (John 20:17). But we may still honour and love them. It is surely proper to remember them by name in our prayers, especially at the Eucharist.

The Epistle to the Hebrews is another rich source of worship material. Both Hebrews and Revelation make clear the calling of believers to serve God as priests (Rev. 5:9–10), continually to offer up to God the sacrifice of praise and to pray for all kinds of people, especially those who suffer.

In worship, we stand at the junction of earth and heaven and intercede on behalf of all those we represent through kinship of one kind or another.

This position of worship is perhaps nowhere better expressed than in Hebrews 12:22–24:

> You have come to Mount Zion, the city of the living God, the heavenly Jerusalem, to myriads of angels, to the full concourse and assembly of the firstborn who are enrolled in heaven, and to God the judge of all, and to the spirits of good men made perfect, and to Jesus the mediator of a new covenant.

PART II

In Private

7

Prayer

The practice of saying prayers is being undermined. Science and theology raise questions about God intervening in the natural order of things. The pace of life in the urban areas where most people now live raises practical problems of finding the time and space for prayer, and in any case most young people have other priorities.

The dominance of science and technology, and the demands of the modern economy, discourage any sense of vocation. Most of us are under increasing pressure to work according to guidelines and schedules laid down by others who themselves are responding to 'the system'.

Under these conditions it is hardly surprising that the regular practice of prayer has disappeared among a majority of British people. In this respect I was interested in the opinion of a leading Islamic Fundamentalist who said that the practice of Islam necessitated an Islamic state. It is easy to see that prayer five times a day cannot be accommodated in the working hours of most secular organizations. Britain at present is having difficulty over Sunday observance.

In this post-Christian society it is necessary to rethink how prayer fits into present-day life. Theological and practical considerations require new understanding and new practices.

It is common among evangelicals to pour scorn on the idea of the religion-less Christianity which was popularized in the sixties. But the phrase was never meant to suggest the demise of public worship and private prayer. On the contrary, the theologians who spoke of religion-less Christianity were committed to liturgical reform and were actively involved in relating the life and teaching of Jesus Christ both to individuals and to society. The advocates of religion-less Christianity were simply proposing that some of the supernatural ways of thinking needed re-evaluating in the light of modern knowledge, and that spirituality needed to be related to people living in a secular society.

From 1964 to 1967 I was an Industrial Chaplain with the South London Industrial Mission whose active Chairman was John Robinson. Bishop John Robinson is best remembered for his book *Honest to God* which made popular a critique of a great deal of traditional Christianity. Stanley Evans, Eric James and Douglas Rhymes were other members of the group of the so-called 'South Bank Theologians'. I knew all these people to be single-minded in their determination to strip away all that obscured the pure vision of God found at the heart of the biblical revelation. They made the brave attempt to convey the meaning of the gospel in language and thought-forms which made sense to people living in a nuclear age. It is perhaps ironic that while these theologians worked hard to relate Christianity to modern society, the hippy movement captured the imagination of large numbers of young people who rejected the values of modern society. Believing Christianity to be spiritually bankrupt these young people turned to Eastern religions for inspiration. The hippy movement was badly shaken when police baton-charged the flower people as they celebrated their free festival in Windsor Great Park. The remnant of the movement has been pursued in recent years as they have attempted to regroup at Stonehenge and in Cwmdu in Wales. The drug scene associated with the hippy movement has given up its quest for psychedelic visions and has become a collection of victims clinging to each other for comfort and dependent upon heroin to ease their pain. Meanwhile, as church-going has continued to decline among the general public, the Charismatic movement has brought new life to growing numbers of believers and congregations.

Many people, disenchanted with politics and sick of the consumer mentality, feel a deep spiritual need.

The temptation for the Church is to try to cash in on this frustration with modern living and call people back to the old traditions. Christian spirituality must not be offered as an antidote to the stresses of modern living. Already a false other-worldliness characterizes much of contemporary religious life. There is talk of love, but the focus is too often upon feelings and only directed towards gaining converts. There is an absence of the this-worldliness of Jesus and of his taking up the Cross on behalf of suffering humanity.

There must be no turning back from new technology, from the quest for international co-operation and from progress towards greater social justice. Spiritual ghettos are not what is required, however attractive they may seem to people facing the harsh realities and immense challenges of the twenty-first century.

When scientific knowledge was restricted and people living in rural communities were more immediately aware of their dependence upon 'nature', it was natural to pray. How else could one hope to alter the weather, ensure good crops or find a cure for disease? Prayer can no longer be thought of as a way of coming to terms with factors beyond our control. Painstaking research and international co-operation are keys to finding solutions to many of our problems. Prayer must be understood as part of these high endeavours, not as a means of opting out.

There is a need among Christians for an understanding of prayer and worship which is not anti-intellectual but leads to genuine engagement in the issues facing us today. We cannot simply revert to the patterns of spiritual life of our forefathers.

One of the valuable insights of the theological debates of the sixties was the proposition that man had 'come of age'. No longer was it appropriate for people to remain in an infant state of helpless dependency upon God. Being created in the image of God and given dominion over the rest of creation, it was proper for the sons and daughters of Adam to use the knowledge of science to solve the problems of daily survival and social organization without constantly asking God for help.

To some, such independence from God seemed to strike at the very roots of religion. It seemed to many that those who were supposed to be the guardians of the holy city were actually demolishing the walls and inviting the secularists in to occupy the temple previously reserved for God.

To others, this recognition of adult status gave them permission to immerse themselves in their work, their art or their political activity without feeling they were usurping God's claim upon their affections or his sovereignty over the universe. Anyone who has sensed divine approval of their autonomy is not going to wish to return to a relationship of tutelage with God.

The story of the Prodigal Son springs to mind. A traditional interpretation of this story would denounce the younger son for asking for his inheritance in advance of his father's death and for then leaving home. The emphasis in this interpretation is upon the sinfulness of wanting independence from the father. But a different interpretation is likely to be nearer the truth. In the time of Jesus and in his society, it was the usual practice for a father to abdicate his ownership of the farm or family business in favour of his sons as soon as they were fully capable of running the enterprise. Exact proportions were laid down for division of the capital among the sons (sorry, males only it seems!) to set them up in their own businesses. The children then had a sacred duty to keep their parents in the manner to which they were accustomed to the best of their ability.

Those who listened to Jesus would not have thought he was advocating continuing dependence upon the head of the family. They would have deplored the recklessness of the younger son in wasting his inheritance, but the focus of the story would have been upon the father's virtue in giving his sons independence and upon his unfailing love towards his wayward son.

I do not think of prayer as some kind of umbilical cord joining us to God; I think of prayer as the communication necessary between working partners (St Paul refers to us being co-workers with Christ). The biblical story of creation specifically gives human beings a role in organizing and developing life on the planet. Our daily work and our leisure pursuits are not a distraction from God, but can be a real outworking of our human vocation. There is much to be said for arranging regular times for prayer, but it can be that a person develops a habit of being continuously in touch with God in a manner which does not require strict adherence to fixed times for personal prayer.

I experience prayer as the intense effort to grasp truth with the aim of authentic and creative activity. When I am preparing a sermon, writing a book, thinking about some aspect of the work of our Kaleidoscope Project, I am trying hard to get at the truth and to communicate that in words or action. Whenever we are single-minded in our concern for the truth we are seeking God and whenever we put this into words or action we are doing the will of God.

I see this process of prayer in the work of an artist. The artist looks carefully at an object to visualize its essential quality. She or he then tries to create something which expresses what has been perceived. I recall an incident when Myfanwy Franks was at work in her studio. A workman interrupted her to attend to some job which needed doing in the room. On the first occasion Myfanwy tolerated the interruption, but on a subsequent occasion when she was hard at work she was so distressed at the interruption that she threw her paintbrushes at the young man, one after another! This expression of artistic temperament is indicative of the intense effort the artist makes to discover and communicate truth.

On another occasion, I helped make the papier-mâché which an artist was using to create a model. It was a revelation to me when the artist explained, 'this is working out bigger than I anticipated'. In other words, the artist is not in control of what is happening: in this case, the artist had to obey his subject. The obedience is what characterizes all true prayer.

In this description of prayer a person does not seek a kind of mental blank, or try hard to put meaning into religious language; rather the individual 'thinks the matter through' and is ready to be committed to action. The insistence upon rational thought and obedient action are characteristics of Puritan spirituality which I think are required in the modern situation where people are given greater opportunities to participate in decision-making.

The emphasis upon rational processes, upon concentrated thinking, does not imply any rejection of the emotional aspects of religion. It implies a passion for truth (or God) and it demands subjugating self-interest.

In this understanding of prayer it is never a form of escapism, nor is it confined to brief periods when rising from sleep or before going to bed. Indeed, it will be found that such prayer is often accomplished at night when the body is at rest and the mind remains active and is most receptive to truth.

The place of Scripture in personal devotions will not be underestimated by anyone who reads the Psalms and the Gospels regularly. Time and time again the Psalms express the raw emotions which are uppermost in our minds and the faith expressed by the Psalmist kindles hope and faithfulness in the reader. The Gospels remind us of the compassion of God, of God's sharing in people's suffering and of his vindication of any life which is dedicated to doing the will of God. Such meditation upon Scripture purifies the mind.

For most of my adult life I have used the lectionary to direct my thoughts to daily readings of Scripture. I strongly recommend this practice, although I recognize that many people may not have sufficient time. I am sure this is a matter churches need to address more seriously by the provision of daily services of worship at times in the morning, at lunchtime, immediately after work and in the evening which would facilitate people being able to hear the Scriptures with great benefit to their spiritual lives.

The recitation of formal prayers, especially the Lord's Prayer, is most beneficial.

The Lord's Prayer reminds us that God is the source, guide and goal of our lives. The reference to heaven reminds us that our mortal lives participate in the eternal life of God. The petition to hallow God's name expresses our concern with truth in every aspect of our lives.

To pray for the coming of God's kingdom and the realization of his will is to ask to see what is below standard in present-day society and to see ways of bringing about change for the better. At the same time, it is to recognize that life on this earth will never reach its full potential, nor will evil be eradicated in the lifespan of any of us. We ask only for the privilege of being involved in a tiny part of the movement forward towards the realization of God's kingdom.

The prayer for daily bread asks for all that is necessary to sustain physical life, while the prayer for forgiveness both for ourselves and those who offend against us asks for all that is necessary to sustain our spiritual life.

'Lead us not into temptation but deliver us from evil' acknowledges the truth that we are always at risk of serious moral and spiritual downfall. We pray for divine assistance to prevent such failure and for deliverance to overcome when we do fall. We place ourselves in the hands of God in the faith that he will deal gently with us. We must not bother too much with what other people think.

The doxology at the end of the Lord's Prayer in which we ascribe sovereignty, power and glory to God testify to the adoration of God which is the beginning and end of prayer.

To adore God is to lose oneself in the immensity of the love of God, to lose anxiety about present things in the light of eternity and to long for union with God who is the source of all life, beauty and truth.

Christian prayer reaches the depths and heights of human experience. We know what it is both to despair and to experience liberation. These encounters with ultimate reality find fullest expression in the death and resurrection of Jesus. When the believer experiences a sense of annihilation, he or she finds their solace in the cross and resurrection of Christ: 'Christ has died, Christ is risen, Christ will come again.' That is why Christians focus in prayer upon a crucifix, the symbol of love at the point of death, or upon an empty cross, the symbol of God's triumph over sin and death. When life is experienced at its extremities, the death and resurrection of Christ make the only sense of our human dilemma. No other meditation is adequate for our need.

Such meditation involves the imagination. Because of a fear of idolatry and superstition many Protestants have been inhibited from using their imagination in their personal devotions. John Bunyan certainly had no such inhibitions, not only is his classic *Pilgrim's Progress* written in the form of allegory, but his other writings also have this visual style. In his spiritual autobiography, *Grace Abounding*, he refers to being 'in a kind of a vision'.

As an example of the use of imagination in personal devotion I would describe the liturgy which takes place in our church on Good Friday. The service is based on the

Stations of the Cross and the Benediction familiar to Catholics. Each year at the time of Lent fourteen of our church members each meditate upon one of the significant events in Christ's journey to the cross. People are invited to express their thoughts in narrative, poetry, music or any other form of communication. At noon on Good Friday we enter the dimly lit chapel and wait in silence. A member of the congregation then announces: 'Today, we come together in the name of Jesus Christ, to meditate on his passion and death in union with the whole Church throughout the world.' There follows the fourteen meditations prepared by the members chosen to do so.

I can testify to the fact that this is one of the rare occasions in public worship when I feel moved to tears. It is not that the meditations are gruesome, it is the profound sense of entering into the sufferings of Christ and of humanity which these imaginative meditations facilitate. Between each meditation we sing a verse of a hymn recalling the sufferings of the mother of Jesus as she is present at the crucifixion of her son. We stand with her, as it were. No mere intellectual grappling with the doctrine of the atonement could bring me into touch with the mystery of Christ's Passion as this service does.

At the end of these meditations we need to turn from contemplations of our Lord's earthly sufferings to meet with our risen Lord and worship him. At other times we would do this by celebrating the Eucharist, but it seems we should abstain from Holy Communion on this day. Perhaps we need to stay a little longer with our Lord's sufferings and express our love to him. On the table before us, covered by a cloth, are bread and wine used at the previous Eucharist. They help fix our attention on the presence with us of our risen Lord Jesus Christ.

We need to wait in expectation for our encounter with God. When Moses went up the mountain he knew he was entering into the presence of God in a special way. The Israelites were afraid of such an encounter with God and waited at the foot of the mountain. We dare not rush into the presence of God and start chatting to him. We wait for the appropriate moment before we uncover the bread and wine.

We sing quietly Thomas Aquinas's hymn:

> Sing, my tongue, the Saviour's glory
> Of his cross the mystery sing; . . .

We come to the fourth verse:

> Low in adoration bending,
> Now our hearts our God revere
> Faith her aid to sight is lending
> Though unseen the Lord is near
> Ancient types and shadows ending,
> Christ our paschal Lamb is here.

The organ stops playing, we wait in total silence, then the President moves to the table, unveils the bread and wine and holds them up for us to see. There follows a few moments of contemplation. There are no words, no movement, just silence as we let our love flow out to our Lord as he comes to us. There follows the blessing, not the usual words given by the President, rather our Lord himself blesses us as the President makes the sign of the cross with the eucharistic bread and wine. I do not think a Protestant congregation could come to this immediately. It follows services of worship where we have become used to using our imaginations as the vehicle of God's encounters with us.

These liturgies can be models for our personal meditations upon the life and words of Jesus.

There is much more that can be said about prayer and I return to this subject in the next chapter, but my present purpose has been to make sense of prayer as an integral part of ordinary living. References in books to so-called 'spiritual giants' ignore the fact that many of them were professional religious people, preachers and mystics who had no secular employment, or writers who gave themselves up to exploration of the spiritual life. Most people have not chosen these priorities, or felt called to them, and it is certain life could not continue if there were not people attending to everyday tasks. Many books on prayer simply create guilt in people who have conflicting priorities. Prayer does not have to fit in to the cramped spaces between domestic responsibilities, working hours and leisure activities. Prayer can be realized in every part of life.

> The trivial round, the common task,
> Will furnish all we ought to ask:
> Room to deny ourselves: a road
> To bring us daily nearer God.
>
> (John Keble)

8

Retreats

The idea of a Retreat does not evoke a positive response from many evangelical Christians. We love conferences and are enthusiastic about week-long assemblies where some of our best speakers are booked to address us. But Retreats are often associated in our minds with the *Spiritual Exercises* of St Ignatius Loyola and this is alien territory for evangelical Protestants. We prefer sitting for prayers and standing up to sing our favourite hymns. Retreats are often held in Roman Catholic monasteries and nothing could be further from our idea of a jolly time.

There are formidable difficulties for evangelicals in going on Retreats which are rooted in the Catholic tradition. It is hard to escape the impression that Ignatius believed in the exercise of the will to overcome the sinful tendencies of the flesh. This really won't do for evangelicals. Indeed, the whole idea of adding anything to the simple acceptance of Jesus as Lord and Saviour would seem to run into the spiritual dangers which Paul dealt with particularly in his Epistle to the Galatians.

It is clear from the New Testament that we receive the Holy Spirit by believing the gospel, not by observing rules or doing exercises. We need to beware of how easily we can turn Christian spirituality into some kind of religious law. We remember Jesus' stern rebuke to the Pharisees who tried to codify the religious life: 'They bind heavy burdens, hard to bear, and lay them on men's shoulders.'

An increasing number of non-Catholics are doing the spiritual exercises of St Ignatius and Retreat directors are becoming sensitive to the needs of Protestants. Some intrepid members of the Reformed tradition have gone into monasteries for 30 days and come out saying it was a remarkable experience. We believe them! Even so, it is an obstacle to most evangelicals that Catholic devotional culture is unfamiliar.

The fact that the Mass is the central feature of daily worship in Catholic Retreat houses of itself creates difficulties for some Protestants, but it is the refusal of Holy Communion which gives the most offence because it calls into question the legitimacy of one's relationship with Christ. I recall an occasion when members of my church joined members of a local Catholic church for a Retreat. When it came to Holy Communion, one of our members burst into tears. She had only recently come to Christian faith and the heart of her conversion experience was the assurance that she was accepted by God. Faced with the refusal of Holy Communion it seemed to her that the priest was in effect denying the truth of her acceptance by God.

A serious problem for evangelicals is the doctrinal content of some Catholic devotional material. It is possible to gloss over this, to hold on to the spirit of the thing without paying too much attention to the words, but this is to miss out on an important element of a Retreat: theological reflection.

As if we have not already said enough, there is one further problem. Retreats are associated in some people's minds with techniques for meditation such as yoga. The 84,000 paths which Buddha taught could lead to enlightenment contrast with the assertion that Jesus is the way, the truth and the life. Withdrawal from the world for three years, three months and three days at a stretch, living a spartan life, rising before 4am and sleeping in upright boxes sounds strenuous; like working for salvation. The fact that some churches welcome inter-faith exploration does not alter the opinion of many evangelicals that these practices have nothing to do with the life and teaching of Jesus. Furthermore, the notion that holiness is achieved by a process of rejecting human nature and the material element of life runs counter to the biblical story of creation and to the New Testament doctrine of incarnation.

With all these psychological and theological hurdles to overcome it may seem somewhat surprising that the members of my church have become enthusiastic about Retreats and many of us make at least one four-day Retreat every year. Let us turn now to a consideration of the main reasons for our commitment to making regular Retreats.

First, we need periods of silence if we are to cultivate the life of the Spirit.

My wife and I were walking up a mountain in the company of a Rumanian Orthodox bishop, Justinian, and a reporter from the BBC. The reporter kept asking the Bishop questions and was recording his answers. The Bishop was clearly reticent and the reporter frustrated. Finally, the reporter asked Justinian: 'How would you suggest I might find God?' The Bishop replied: 'Stop talking.'

I am obliged to Kenneth Leech in his book *Spirituality and Pastoral Care* for this early testimony to the place of silence in the Christian life found in the writings of

Ignatius of Antioch, a contemporary of the New Testament.

> It is better to keep quiet and be, says Ignatius, than to be fluent and not be. He speaks of the silences of Jesus, and links the attainment of silence with 'full spiritual maturity' (Eph. 15). He claims that the three major events in the work of salvation — the virginity of Mary, the incarnation, and the death of Christ —were brought to pass in 'the deep silence of God', that is, in the depths of God's being (Eph. 19). Christ himself is described as the Word who proceeds from silence (Magn. 8). Thus anyone who would enter into the depths of God's mysterious activity and of his very being must begin to practise a theology of silence.

Living on what is virtually a traffic island, it is very difficult for staff at Kaleidoscope to experience silence. I am quite clear that when many of us come to the point of exhaustion it is not that we have been working too hard, it is a case of stimulus fatigue. We can no longer think straight because of people calling out to us, the telephone calls from outside, the constant sight and sound of people trying to catch our attention.

This matter of no longer being able to think straight, a common complaint, requires more than several minutes silence. It requires prolonged stretches of silence over a period of three or four days.

To begin with, silence is hard to handle. Our mind will simply not be quiet. And then when we try to be still the exercise seems pointless. We do not experience any word or vision from God. We wait impatiently. It is at this point that we must believe that God is in the silence and that the Holy Spirit is preparing our hearts to receive him. From then on, it is simply a matter of opening oneself to God, feeling the ground beneath us and the air and warmth around us and knowing that God is good.

Once we start thinking straight we may find ourselves in trouble. We may face the knowledge of our sinfulness, or we may face the reality of our comparative insignificance. Do we really matter in this world? We must struggle with these thoughts and perhaps the peace of God will come to us as a gift. If not, this is where we have need of a spiritual director. The director of the Retreat should be able to help us in our struggle.

Secondly, we want the experience of daily Eucharist, sharing a common life and eating together (Acts 2:46). Most Christians experience this spiritual friendship within the weekly programme of church activities, in house groups in the case of Charismatic churches, or in the home Eucharists which are a feature of our own church. We want to deepen this friendship in Christ by means of some days together where we share worship and life in the family of the Church.

Thirdly, we need time for theological reflection. Many of the themes of Christian faith cannot be taught, still less can they be experienced, by means only of sermons. Free Churches used to have mid-week services for Bible study and prayer. Unfortunately, these are no longer regular features of modern-day church life. Nor is it satisfactory that meetings for celebration should replace theological study. We need some hours together to ponder upon a theological theme with the help of someone in the group with a knowledge of theology. Without theological discipline faith lacks a firm intellectual base.

Fourthly, we perceive a great pastoral need for spiritual

direction. This is particularly true in the area of personal morality. Many spiritual problems have a moral element. The last thing which is required is for the preacher to denounce sin from the pulpit in a way which seems to condemn the sinner. I remember an occasion when a preacher denounced abortion without any qualification or apparent compassion. A woman in the front suddenly got up and rushed out of the church sobbing. I condemn that preacher; my prayers go out to that woman.

Pastoral ministry cannot be conducted from a pulpit. The hallmark of the ministry of Jesus is that he drew near to people and was approachable. He was able in this way to understand their personal moral problems without having to make generalized statements.

It is particularly unhelpful that the Church seems to want to lay down the law in matters of sexual morality. Ask a Church spokesperson to give a commentary on the many items in a newspaper and there will be a marked degree of reticence to make public pronouncements on all these complicated issues. But, if there is a reference to sex outside of marriage, homosexuality, abortion, rising divorce rates or illegitimacy, then there is the likelihood of categorical statements sounding very much like laws. And we know the law condemns. A woman who has had an abortion knows she is the wrong side of the law in many churches. A person who is homosexual fears that any meaningful expression of his sexuality will bring him under condemnation. Pre-marital sex, even within a stable and loving relationship, is contrary to traditional moral teaching. Such moral issues are the source of guilt and spiritual isolation which burden many people.

Jesus showed reticence in condemning sinners, even notorious ones 'caught in the act'. When they brought an adulterous woman to Jesus, he made no comment, he wrote in the sand and told the person without sin to cast the first stone.

A personal Retreat provides an occasion for such sensitive and liberating ministry. This process of self-examination, confession of sin, sorrow for wrongdoing and absolution is central to the work of Retreats. This pastoral ministry is sanctioned by Scripture. It is exemplified in the ministry of Jesus who pronounced the forgiveness of sins to those who were penitent. Whatever problems there may be in interpreting the words of Jesus in Matthew 16:18–19 and 18:15–18, there can be no doubt that Christ gave authority to the Apostles to pronounce the forgiveness of sins in his name.

In the Gospels it is recorded specifically that the Church is to continue Christ's ministry of forgiving sins. The Holy Spirit is given to the Church precisely for this purpose (John 20:22). The writer of the First Epistle of John acknowledges the need for a regular ministry of confession and absolution. Christians who should not sin, do so. In view of this it is vitally important that sins should be confessed in the confidence that God will forgive in accordance with his covenant and on the basis of Christ's atoning sacrifice (1 John 1:3).

Evangelicals reserve the word 'sacrament' with respect to baptism and the Eucharist only, but that does not indicate a rejection of confession as an essential feature of Christian discipline. It is usual to include a prayer of confession in services of public worship in addition to the petition for forgiveness in the Lord's Prayer. The reference in the Epistle of James (James 5:16) indicates that confession was usual in the early Church, although what is recommended would appear to be an acknowledgement of faults to one another and not to a superior person. Evangelicals reject Catholic teaching that the imparting of absolution is reserved to the ordained priest. Clearly it is necessary, however, to be sure that a confessor is a person who can be trusted and one who has sufficient spiritual understanding never to be shocked by a confession.

The truth is that we have all got ourselves into a sinful mess and need to find ways of admitting this without fear of rejection. I have found it helpful when giving comfort or counsel to a penitent person to invite them to receive Holy Communion immediately following confession so that they know they are counted worthy through the grace of our Lord Jesus Christ.

Many members of my church now book at least one four-day Retreat a year at our Retreat House, Pencilmaren, in Wales. A quarter of a mile from the road, approached through a bracken covered rocky hillside, Pencilmaren nestles in the fold of the hills, a place apart. It is a stone and slate Welsh farmhouse with three barns, one of which has been made into a small but beautiful chapel. Surrounding the house are gardens and 147 acres of sheep pasture.

The daily worship focuses on three services: a morning Eucharist, and meditations at noon and at nightfall. There are periods of silence and short meditations upon Bible readings. For people living in an urban setting and those who work at Kaleidoscope these Retreats give a time of rest and peace with the opportunity to remind ourselves of the beauty of creation. We usually include a visit to the coast and some other place of outstanding natural beauty nearby.

In the evening in the house as we sit around the log fire we share together in theological reflection. The important theme of one Retreat is the Holy Trinity. This is a doctrine of first importance but might be the theme of only one Sunday's sermon in a year. How can a preacher expound on this theme in a sermon of reasonable length? Either, the sermon will be hopelessly overloaded, or else the treatment of the subject will be trivial. A four-day Retreat centred on our experience of God, Father, Son and Holy Spirit gives us the time and space to glorify God and to contemplate the mystery of his Being. It also provides us with some hours of thinking together about the meaning of this doctrine and an opportunity to correct common notions such as: Jesus the God-man who is nothing like any of us, or: the Holy Spirit like some substance poured out on us so that we are either full, half full or empty! We need time to grasp the truth about relationships which is seen most completely in the true doctrine of God. These are matters which require time both for meditation in the chapel and for careful thinking and talking together with an input from someone with theological knowledge.

The theme of another Retreat might be the Eucharist. Bishop John Robinson wrote a commentary on the Eucharist with the title *Liturgy Coming to Life*. It is an account of liturgical experiment in a Cambridge College and describes how the Holy Communion came to life for many members of that community. Every church can make a similar attempt to 'do' the four actions of the Eucharist in such a way as to bring out the meaning of this central and creative act of worship. This too needs time both for meditation and discussion with theological input. Four days is not too long.

It is not a contradiction of radical theology and the kind of extrovert spirituality we are advocating that we should be attracted to a spiritual discipline which is not unlike that associated with monasticism.

Walter Rauschenbusch (1861–1918), the American Baptist who radically re-oriented theology in America, was known as the 'father of the social gospel'. As a pastor in the 'Hell's Kitchen' area of New York City he became aware of the social and economic problems of working people and their families. Distressed by harsh treatment, unsanitary health conditions, child labour and similar problems, Rauschenbusch became convinced that the message of Jesus applied to society as well as to individuals. He set out his distinctive views in two powerful books, *Christianity and the Social Crisis* and *A Theology for the Social Gospel*. The central message of Jesus as he understood it was the kingdom of God. He understood this kingdom not just as a future eschatological state, but as potentially present in human society. He urged the Church to become involved in society so as to bring society closer to the ideal of the kingdom of God.

It is interesting that this father of the social gospel advocated a spiritual discipline similar to that of the Catholic Jesuits. He founded the Brotherhood of the Kingdom, a voluntary association which would endeavour to realize the ethical and spiritual principles of Jesus both in their individual and social aspects. There can be no doubt of the need for this union of social action and spiritual discipline in the Church today.

Spirituality must not become a substitute for hard thinking and social action. A growth in mere pietism would be disastrous for progress towards social justice and international peace. The 'Nonconformist conscience' which influenced national life in a previous generation was not concerned only with personal morality but threw a

spotlight on political morality. Without this political morality public debate becomes an auction in which people are
invited to vote for the benefits on offer. Such national
self-indulgence is a contradiction of the responsible social
relationships enshrined in the Old and New Testaments.

Retreats are of special value to people who are conscious
of being at a critical point in life. These times typically
occur in late adolescence, a few years into marriage, at
mid-life and at the onset of old age. At other times we are
often too busy to think about what is happening to us.
Examinations, marriage, making a home, the birth and
early rearing of children and the demands of a career: all
these things keep us fully occupied. Suddenly, life catches
us unawares and we find ourselves out of our depth.
We need to get away, sometimes urgently, to think. We
unexpectedly find it necessary to re-examine our values,
our lifestyle and what meaning we attach to our existence.
A Retreat is of special relevance then, particularly if the
spiritual director is a person of appropriate experience
and skill. In these circumstances, we need an individually
guided Retreat with the stated expectation of spiritual
guidance or counselling. A telephone conversation will
usually confirm if we have found the right place.

It is well-known that a Retreat is not always initially a
comfortable experience. Our confidence in life sometimes
takes a nose dive, or circumstances take control over us
and we experience darkness. Mystics speak of 'the dark
night of the soul', others refer to the *via negativa*. These
are technical terms for very common experiences. To begin
with, facing up to this overwhelming sense of lostness
can be painful. But after a time there comes a sense of
relief and light begins to appear. As we wait upon God a
new sense of direction is born and we regain our energy.

I do not mean that our circumstances appear to improve, but we receive a sense of well-being. This peace of God should always accompany faith but sometimes it comes as a surprise to us that we find joy even in distressing circumstances.

A Retreat can last anything from a weekend to 40 days, but the full menu can only be stomached by people with a large spiritual appetite. Spiritual appetite is not confined to church-goers. The work of Kaleidoscope was undertaken by some of the key members of my church, but we would never have succeeded without the input of half a dozen young people who had difficulty relating to church life but who had big spiritual appetites. Many young people who go to Taizé find the spiritual life of that religious community is what, unknowingly, they have been searching for.

Churches do not always have a wide enough understanding of spiritual life and require a particular kind of commitment which not everyone is ready to make. Retreats often provide a more flexible response to the needs of individuals and can be the pathway towards a deeper understanding of the Bible, the sacraments and life in the Spirit.

Children and retreats

It is sometimes mistakenly assumed that because children do not understand abstract thought, they cannot have a valid experience of God. Of course, this contradicts the teaching of Jesus. We have not found it successful to have children attending Retreats which are for adults, but we have had good experience of running Retreats especially for children.

It is estimated that only about 15 per cent of British children attend church regularly. In this situation there will be strong peer pressure not to be in the minority of church attenders. Many sport and recreational activities take place on Sundays and visits to friends and family are becoming an established pattern for many. What is the Christian family to do in these circumstances?

I believe that Christian parents must not be shy of explaining that because of their faith they want to worship regularly and in that respect they are a Christian family. When the children are old enough, they can decide for themselves.

In many churches provision is made for children in Sunday school and Junior Church. There is a danger, more in Free Churches perhaps than others, of taking children out of family worship and providing a substitute which will not be satisfactory for long. Children can and do absorb more than we think of liturgy and worship and many want to be included in the worshipping family of the Church. There is no reason why they should not read their own books or draw during the sermon!

Children enjoy special events and a four-day residential Retreat is popular. Firstly, there is the excitement of going away with your friends and doing something special. Pencilmaren has the advantage of being in the Welsh hills and provides acres of land to be explored, streams to be dammed and trees to climb. In addition to freedom and fun, games played and stories told around the log fire in the evening, there is a serious content and structure to the day. Morning and evening prayers are said in the small stone chapel and the reverence of the children is inspiring. I recall how after a longer afternoon at the sea than planned, Pippa, aged six, was packed off to bed before the evening prayers. When she realized that she was missing out she gave a howl of protest and so, wrapped in blankets, she joined her older friends in the candle-lit chapel!

The children are divided into appropriate age groups and work with an adult in understanding and preparing for next Sunday's worship at church. The Eucharist is the focus and the children's understanding of this mystery is astounding. Eucharistic prayers are prepared by the children.

On one occasion, the younger children, helped by the others, made a collage of creation to be presented at the table with the bread and wine. The one from the sea containing dead crabs, lobster claws and shrimps could be smelled as well as seen! On Sunday the children returned to the church and led the service, taking an active part in the Eucharist. They impressed everyone with their reverence and competence.

Our experience at Pencilmaren would lead us to advocate a Retreat as a normal and necessary part of a maturing Christian life. We would urge churches to build links with appropriate Retreat centres in order to renew their worship and empower their members more effectively to go about the work of the kingdom of God in their neighbourhoods.

PART III

In Public

9

Extrovert Spirituality

Josephine Bax in her book *Meeting God Today* used the phrase 'extrovert spirituality' to describe the Christian experience of those who find their attention focused on issues such as peace and justice, community life and poverty. It is unscientific to draw too sharp a distinction between introvert and extrovert types because both tendencies reside in all of us. In religious life it is true that many of those most active in work among the poor find their motivation and energy from their contemplation of Christ. The phrase 'extrovert spirituality' is helpful because it acknowledges the validity of an understanding of mission which is not primarily concerned with church life but looks outward to the life of the world. Clearly these alternatives are not in conflict, they belong together, but everyone can see there is a difference between those forms of mission which aim at bringing people into the Church and those which aim at overcoming injustice, disadvantage or disease.

The annual report will usually indicate the primary aim of an organization. In the case of a church, does the report give the number of converts, baptisms and new members; or does the report describe areas of work and people helped without reference to their religious status?

The phrase 'extrovert spirituality' which I am pleased Josephine Bax used to describe the orientation of my church refers to a mission primarily directed at reducing the sufferings of people addicted to heroin and other drugs. We do not narrow our concern to their need, but we serve them regardless of their motivation or responsiveness to the gospel.

The justification for such unconditional caring is the unconditional love of God. Christ proclaimed liberation to all who were in prison, he brought healing to the sick and gave food to the multitude; and to those who came seeking he gave the secret of the kingdom of God (Matt. 13:11). Bread to the many who are hungry and faith to the few who are seeking is the definitive model for Christian mission.

Extrovert spirituality has deep roots in church worship and personal devotion to Christ. It is difficult to sustain radical work without strong faith because invariably you meet opposition from powerful elements in society who wish to maintain a differential between themselves and those they despise and oppress. Although people acknowledge the 'deserving poor', the dominant opinion is that people who suffer 'have only themselves to blame'.

For a brief period after the War there was a vision of a Welfare State, but the idea was soon abandoned because it did not strike hard-working people as fair that the unemployed, large families, foreigners, the sick and the old should all enjoy a standard of living not far below that of decent folk who work. The Thatcher government believed that it was right to increase the rewards to the entrepreneurs who create wealth and that it was necessary to reduce State benefits to people who it was perceived did not really need them. The prevailing mood has been hostile towards those who are the outcasts of society.

Illicit drug users are the least loved members of society. I recall the remark of a police officer who had been harrassing my clients: 'You may not like it, 500 people may protest, but 50,000 people out there approve of what we're doing.' He rightly judged public opinion.

Anyone working for a radical cause will understand the difficulties. I do not think it would be possible to mobilize a church membership consisting of a cross-section of people from the community to undertake unrewarding community work unless that congregation had a deep spirituality.

Quite simply: Kaleidoscope would not exist without the gospel and the Eucharist. When we make the offering in church we offer up to God everything he has created and the whole human enterprise. When we make the eucharistic prayer we consecrate not only the bread on the Holy table but the whole of life. When we break the bread we see Christ being broken and his life being offered up for the salvation of the world. When we receive the bread and the wine, it is for us the body and blood of Christ making us his disciples sent into the world to serve.

Kaleidoscope was born out of the preaching of the gospel. It is possible to read the New Testament as if it were an evangelistic tract. You can see the dozen or so most appropriate verses displayed on sandwich boards carried through the streets of cities and towns by evangelists, or you can see the same texts printed on advertisements in buses and trains. But what is the picture of Jesus we see when we read the New Testament as a whole?

Jesus spoke words of forgiveness and performed healing miracles out of his compassion for people. The crucifixion of Jesus is evidence of individual sin by those involved in plotting against him and acquiescing to his execution, but it is also evidence of moral corruption in the State. There was an unholy alliance between the Jewish hierarchy and the Roman authorities, there were irregularities in the trial proceedings including false evidence, the soldiers humiliated and tortured Jesus and the whole society gave support to the barbaric practice of crucifixion. There was both individual and institutional sin. St Paul describes sin as corrupting the whole of life, even sapping the good which people intend to do (see Rom. 7). The implication is that the followers of Jesus will find themselves in a wideranging ministry of courageous opposition to much that is wrong in the world. The followers of Jesus will always have compassion for the victims of our sinful society.

The resurrection is for believers the proof that God vindicates those who stand for truth and will ensure the ultimate triumph of good over evil. This is a matter of faith: there is no scientific justification for believing in human progress. The resurrection appearances of Jesus convinced the Apostles that Christ was present in them by the Holy Spirit, sending them out to proclaim liberation in the name of God and to demonstrate the kingdom of God. Churches with a knowledge of Christ's resurrection must be local demonstrations of the kingdom of God. These need to be public demonstrations bringing actual change both in individuals and in the community.

Not everyone working at Kaleidoscope is a professing Christian, but I detect in all of them the work of the Holy Spirit. Perhaps I have caught something of Orthodox spirituality that discerns the work of the Holy Spirit in all people by virtue of being created by God, and not only in those who profess faith in Christ.

One of the clearest examples of demonstrations of the kingdom of God is the hospice movement. There is much evidence that modern secular society is embarrassed by death and that many medical professionals share this embarrassment. Those Christian doctors, nurses and Religious sisters who pioneered skilled and creative treatment with those suffering terminal disease demonstrate the outworking of Christian faith.

Let me comment further that the practical outworking is where the pain is. Even in something as obviously beneficial as a hospice, there will be opposition to be overcome. The local general hospital will not always want to transfer patients, even if the dying person and the relatives want this. There are financial implications, there is the implied criticism of the care of the general hospital and there are the technical problems of linking statutory to non-government services. There is the chore of fund-raising. There are legal problems, planning problems, not to mention everyday management problems. Why get involved? It is easier to preach the gospel from the Bible. This is why so much church life is anodyne.

Many Christians have become aware of the necessity for the Church to become more involved in the life of the world. There is talk of a need of 'an appropriate spirituality' which will effectively embrace both our experience of God and our experience of the world. There is talk of the need to strike a proper balance between spirituality and social action. An earnest Christian speaks of her difficulty in taking her faith into her work. These concerns show a presupposition that God is in the Church and in the hearts of believers, but needs to be taken from these holy places to the world beyond! This is not simply theological error, it is symptomatic of a kind of spiritual schizophrenia in which a person has a self-consciousness of God which is somehow disconnected from reality outside. We are made out of the dust of the earth, we do not exist without the world outside of ourselves, there is no point where we cease and the world outside begins.

For first generation Christians and for those who accept the historic creeds of the Church, even our future state is a 'resurrection of the body'. There is no such reality as a disembodied soul — at least not in Christian theology. The distinctive revelation of the New Testament is incarnation — God in flesh.

You cannot hold a proper balance between spiritual life and social action. Spirituality which is not socially active is a dead spirituality.

It is a terrible deficiency of some Protestant theology that there is a denial of natural theology. The belief that our minds have become so clouded by sin that we cannot recognize truth if it is shown to us makes any rational thinking and discussion pointless. It is right to assert that we cannot find God by rational argument alone, but it is wrong to say that we are quite incapable of recognizing the truth in any description of reality. Quite simply, a person can see the truth in the life and teaching of Jesus. We may agree that it will need the Holy Spirit to draw a person out of his self-centredness, to enable someone to respond in faith to Christ, but we do not need to say to a seeker after truth: 'There is nothing I can say to you that will make any sense, just kneel there praying for a revelation.' Such advice would open the door to an altogether illusory kind of religious experience. Matthew Fox in his book *Original Blessing* has rightly argued that man's creation in the image of God takes precedence over man's original sin. We are created in the image of God, and although the image may have been shattered by sin, the pieces have not all been thrown away!

Natural theology, the belief that we have some natural ability to recognize God, is the bridge between our ordinary, everyday knowledge and our religious experience. It is this which enables us to see in the world around us and in all of life that God is present and active.

It is unlikely that we shall develop an appropriate spirituality which can embrace both our experience of God and our experience of the world while we hold to a theology which puts all the emphasis on a revelation of God and has little to say positively about our everyday living. For one thing, we shall completely fail to give any priority to ecological issues if we are preoccupied with our own salvation and largely indifferent to God's creation. We shall not find an appropriate spirituality until we discover an appropriate theology.

I like the definition of spirituality given by Sister Lavinia Byrne, lecturer at Heythrop College, quoted by Josephine Bax:

By spirituality I understand how we live out of what we believe. What we believe is our theology and everybody has one, and how we live out of it, our daily living, is our spirituality, because we are trying to live with meaning.

Renewed theology has required liturgical renewal. It is evident in the liturgies of recent years that the heavy emphasis upon sin has been replaced by a stronger emphasis on the goodness of God. This change of emphasis may not be as apparent in the spontaneous prayers familiar in Free Churches. It is noticeable that in evangelical services of Holy Communion, the prayers of thanksgiving often focus exclusively on the death of Christ. When Jesus gave thanks during the Last Supper he gave thanks for bread and wine as the fruits of the earth which sustain physical life and for the redemption to be obtained by the offering up of his body and blood. We must learn to give thanks to God for all he has done, not only for what he has done for us. This thanksgiving for creation and redemption can be the beginning of a recovery of an appropriate spirituality which is both individual and social, both intimate and public.

Perhaps the opening words of a Catholic eucharistic prayer are a good illustration of praise to God for all his works:

Praise to the Father
Father, you are holy indeed,
and all creation rightly gives you praise.
All life, all holiness comes from you
through your Son, Jesus Christ our Lord,
by the working of the Holy Spirit.
From age to age you gather a people to yourself,
so that from east to west
a perfect offering may be made
to the glory of your name.

(*Eucharistic Prayer III*)

That theology affects the way we live is clear to me from my own childhood experience. My family life at home before evacuation in the War was very happy. In retrospect I can see that my father's upbringing in the Christian Brethren was both beneficial and harmful. The Christian

106

ideals I was taught and the faith I later received have been a lifelong blessing, but I needed to free myself from some of the extreme theology which so badly inhibited my father. Because of an almost paranoic fear of the depravity of the world, my father could only enjoy those things which could be labelled 'Christian'. He avoided staying in any house unless it was a 'Christian' home. He would go to hear the London Evangel Choir because it sang sacred music. There was anxious comment when my aunt was urged by her music teacher to sing some classical music by secular composers. My uncle obtained exemption from the Closed Shop agreement in his industry on religious grounds because it was his belief that membership of a trade union would bind him to a non-Christian organiz-ation. Another uncle forbade his children to celebrate Christmas because it was a festival not explicitly sanc-tioned by Scripture. When my father opened a radio shop, people in the Assembly questioned whether radio was an invention of the Devil; he was advised that haberdashery would be a more suitable retail trade. I remember my own difficulty whenever we sang a line of the hymn:

> Take my voice and let me sing,
> Always, only, for my King.

I tried hard not to sing any popular songs during my adolescence!

My father and I, to a lesser extent, were both socially crippled by this theology. I know from this experience that an exaggerated understanding of total depravity and the degenerate nature of unredeemed man makes it diffi-cult for some conservative evangelical Christians to relate constructively to the world.

St Paul was never in any doubt about the corruption of the world by sin, but he knew of God's plan of salvation that he would bring the universe, everything in heaven and on earth, into a unity in Christ. This is the vision which inspires a comprehensive mission to the world.

10

Christian Lifestyle

It may be assumed that a Christian will want to live a life consistent with the teaching of Jesus. St Matthew's Gospel is clearly intended to make the words and actions of Jesus authoritative for the Christian community, and Chapters five to seven of that Gospel, the Sermon on the Mount, set out the ethics of Christian discipleship.

It is not easy, however, to deduce the lifestyle of a Christian from the Sermon on the Mount. Admittedly it seems that Matthew is giving us a new law to replace the Old Testament commandments, but in fact the precepts of Jesus are not intended to be understood legalistically, as prescribing what Christians must do in all circumstances. Similarly, the demands of love may require that you do not retaliate if someone slaps you on the face, or again the demands of love may require you to go much further in generosity than the law requires. The teaching on prayer is not meant to provide fixed sentences for recitation but is illustrative of the conversation the believer may have with God. The believer is urged not to be anxious but this does not mean that the disciple should not be prudent in business.

Bishop John Robinson sums it up:

The Sermon on the Mount does not say in advance, 'This is what in any given circumstances you must do', but 'This is the kind of thing which at any moment, if you are open to the absolute, unconditional will of God, the kingdom (or love) can demand of you.' (*Honest to God*, p. 111)

Is there anything authentically Christian which should distinguish believers from non-believers?

Methodists used to be total abstainers, although this is no longer true for all of them. Baptists still use non-alcoholic wine at Holy Communion, but most of them now will accept a glass of wine at a dinner party.

Smoking is bad for health and so it is contrary to the belief that one's body is the temple of the Holy Spirit. But the same can be said of drinking some tap water, or living in a town centre where levels of air pollution are high. Absolute rules can hardly be applied.

Gambling can certainly be a form of addiction. But does God withhold his blessing from the Catholic Church because of their Christmas draws, or their football pools? If not, is God condoning the practice?

The Anabaptists were pacifists and the Quakers still are. This must surely be right? Well, not all Christians agree about the justification for the Falklands War or the Gulf War. Perhaps we can all agree that Dr Robert Runcie rightly judged that a service of thanksgiving after war should not be an occasion of patriotic pride. There does seem to have been a turning away from vulgar jingoism.

Perhaps simplicity could be the hallmark of Christian discipleship. This should not be confused with opting for cheap alternatives. Indeed the search for cheap alternatives is at the heart of the consumer mentality.

My wife and I spent time in a Rumanian Orthodox monastery. Since the monastery was on top of a high mountain, we were a huge distance from the troubled world of the rest of Rumania. We ate off fine plates, the food was plentiful, well-prepared and served carefully. The gardens could be featured in a television programme they were so lovely. The library was well-stocked with ancient and modern books of theology and other good literature. The church was richly decorated but without much furniture, which is the Orthodox style. There was a museum of religious relics, chalices, icons, illuminated manuscripts and exquisitely embroidered cloths. The toilet was out of this world, being a hole in a plank suspended over the side of the mountain with a drop of thousands of feet!

I think this monastery was a good model for a Christian community. Nothing was shoddy, everything was orderly, meal times were either a fast or a feast and the produce was fresh from their immaculate vegetable gardens.

While we were there a nun died. We were all crowded into her room. She was dressed in her best habit. In her dying hour she was surrounded by love and upheld in prayer. But the atmosphere was not artificial: one novice clung to her and wept profusely; at one point a dog was held up for her inspection because she loved dogs. Sacramental oils alternated with medicines. She died in a bare room with only the adornments of her religion decorating the walls, but she died richly.

I dare not compare our attempt to create a Christian community at Kaleidoscope, but I can say we have made an attempt. We did not specify the cheapest materials although our architect had no money or extravagance. We chose copper for the roof because the life expectancy of cheaper materials was not long. I once wrote a paper for a seminar of the United Nations organization who visited Kaleidoscope. In it I described our aim:

> At the Kaleidoscope club and hostel we are trying to return to more basic ideas about living with an emphasis on 'farmhouse' food, authentic decoration and fittings, and simple, unostentatious hospitality. We have this conviction that people need a place they can return to, where they are sure of acceptance and warmth, where the only condition attached to their welcome is that they are not intent on destroying the place.

I have stated our intentions, but no doubt we are inconsistent at many points and I only refer to this statement to give concrete meaning to the principle of simplicity.

Many people give conscientious thought to certain features of modern-day living in a consumer society. They are right to question the motives for many of our purchases; do we buy for usefulness or for status? They try to avoid purchasing goods which perpetuate the exploitation of people. They try to have regard to ecology in every aspect of their living. These are surely clear principles we should all be guided by, but I can't go along with those who admonish us to buy cars only for their utility and clothes only to meet our needs. I love my Morgan car and it is for me a work of art. I wear a nearly white pullover and old pair of trousers when I go down to the Kaleidoscope club on a Friday night, but otherwise I wear more formal clothes of good quality. I hope I don't choose clothes with too much intention to impress, but I certainly don't choose them simply to keep warm or avoid being arrested for indecent exposure!

We have been dealing only with the superficial marks of a Christian lifestyle. The truly spiritual person cannot be identified simply by reference to these marks and it is hard to point to single features of their personality which impress me. But we have all met individuals who have a certain serenity and simple honesty and goodness which we admire. Their integrity is diamond hard and just as clear. Who can tell from which spiritual depths they have drawn their strength? But in some cases we happen to know of their life of prayer and worship.

You can't make a flower pretty. All you can do is water it if needed and feed it if it requires a richer soil. Otherwise, in the main leave it alone. I am sure the same is true for human beings. If they are malnourished and denied the basic necessities of care they will not thrive well, but all people have a beauty of their own. It only needs love to bring this out. That is the problem. Where do we find love?

In more cases than we care to know, love has been denied in childhood. Because I work with young people in need of care it seems to me sometimes that everyone has been deprived and abused, but of course that is not generally true. Even so, there are circumstances in most people's lives when it seems that love has been withdrawn. To a child this may seem to be the case when their mother goes into hospital. To some of us at my age it seemed a bit like that when we went away because of evacuation in the War. To others it is like that through bereavement, or through a messy divorce. There are many circumstances in life where we seem to be cut off from love, rejected, or betrayed.

113

Our security cannot rest entirely within our own resources or in other people who may change or die. We need to find that much deeper serenity which H. H. Price has attributed to the spiritual person: 'A spiritual person feels himself to be "more at home" in the universe than unspiritual persons do.' That deeper security can only be found in God.

I recall a young woman in our hostel who was crying and could not be consoled. She felt she had been tricked into having her first baby adopted and thought everyone was trying to manipulate her into making the same decision for the baby she was carrying. She could not see that anyone loved her, and as she recalled her life history she came to the conclusion that God had cursed her. I listened for a long time because I could see the justice in her accusation. Before I left her, I asked if she thought Jan had been kind to her and if she found the hostel of some benefit. I told her a little of the story of how the church had struggled to build the hostel and provide for its running. I explained to her that I believed this was a response to the will of God. 'My conclusion is that God loves you', I said to her.

I am sure not many of our clients come to that conclusion and I am glad in a way they do not. I would not want them to feel a sense of obligation. I think when we are still for a moment we can all come to realize that God loves us. Look at creation, breathe deeply, taste clear water, feel the earth, listen to the sounds of the universe if you can cut out the sounds of machines where you are. 'Feeling at home in the universe' is partly a matter of getting to know the place and learning of the love of the Father.

You cannot tell people these things without sounding

trite. We must all discover these truths slowly. Some old people know these things, but others struggle to hold on to their wits and their belongings, afraid to die.

There is a *via negativa* — a negative way. It sounds dreadful, and in a way it is, but it can lead to light and peace if you hold on to your faith in God. The *via negativa* is when you come to a 'no entry' sign in life. It is the end of a love affair; it is bereavement; it is redundancy and unemployment; it is bad health; it is time to leave the home; it is the end of an era.

Take only one step at a time. It is dangerous walking in the dark. Keep praying even though it seems no one is there. Think only this, 'I must keep going on'. Put your trust in God. Not soon, but in time you will come through the darkness. You will one day find your spirits lift. You will have won your victory.

Struggle has a social dimension. This presents a difficult challenge for the Church because this introduces political questions which divide the membership of any local church. The temptation is to avoid these issues, but that is to allow the status quo to go unchallenged, which assumes we have already reached a state near to the king-dom of God on earth. Christians must be in the forefront of change until God's kingdom is fully realized.

My own awakening to the need for political involvement came in 1960 when I first became aware of the struggle of the African people in Angola. I think until then I naively assumed that Western colonial regimes were on the whole benevolent. Then I read of atrocities committed by Afri-cans against Europeans. There were claims that these atro-cities were committed by terrorists directed by Communists. That seemed to be the general opinion in Britain at the time. It was certainly the view of Her

Majesty's Government. Some businessmen returning from Angola gave a different account. Then Clifford Parsons, a respected Baptist missionary, broke the customary silence and gave a terrible indictment of the Portuguese colonial administration in Angola. Government sources denied this version of events and stressed that Portugal was Britain's oldest ally.

As conflicting reports appeared in the newspapers and even the basic facts were in dispute, it occurred to me that the truth could be discovered by taking the editor of the *Observer* newspaper to meet the first missionary arriving in Britain from Angola. It was rather unfair of us to intercept this poor woman as she came off the plane, obviously worn out from the long journey and her previous harrowing experiences. As we pressed her for information, she struggled with her conscience because of her commitment to the missionary society not to get involved in political matters. Her commitment to truth and humanity overcame this inhibition and she soon gave us a full account of the injustices and terrors of the colonial regime in Angola. I could hardly control my temper.

I had been joined at this time by two ministerial colleagues, George Thompson Brake and Len Addicott, and together we formed the Angola Action Group. In August 1961, I accompanied Mr George Thomas MP, later to become Viscount Tonypandy, on a fact-finding mission to the Congo–Angola border. We were assisted by experienced missionaries who knew the terrain and the native languages well. They took us to remote spots on the border where we could interview Africans as they came out from Angola. These refugees told horrifying stories of atrocities and institutionalized oppression and violence. We checked the veracity of their stories carefully by reference to others who had come by a different route from the same areas. When we returned to Britain we published our findings and campaigned for the liberation of the Angolan people. I am glad to state that the Churches in the main believed our report and pressurized the British Government to cease supporting Portugal in this conflict. In this way, Christians took part in a historic struggle and made a small but significant contribution to Angola achieving independence.

In the Sermon on the Mount the disciple of Jesus is described as someone who hungers and thirsts to see right prevail (Matt. 5:6). This is often interpreted in terms of an individual's relationship to God, but we can also give a wider interpretation. The disciple of Jesus is the one who in the midst of the world's hopelessness is continually encouraging, helping to overcome obstacles, co-operating with others to obtain better conditions for living. This is the struggle to bring about the kingdom of God on earth now, in ways that make visible God's eternal world.

11

Let Be

In the first chapter I described the loss of a pattern of spirituality known to generations of evangelical Christians. I described a sense of homelessness which many people feel due to the radical changes taking place in the Church today. I have tried to give permission to people to find new expressions of Christian faith and in the chapter on Retreats especially I have recognized that spirituality is a process of discovering who we are in the providence of God and having permission to be fully ourselves. I understand spirituality as the response we make to God in our personal lives and in our efforts to realize God's kingdom on earth.

I have given attention to the traditional elements of Christian worship emphasizing the central importance of the Word and sacraments without which worship can become superficial with neither roots going down into the bedrock of historic faith nor branches reaching out into the wider community. I turn now to a consideration of the mission of the Church in contemporary society. Throughout this book I have described an understanding of spirituality which is outward looking and expressed in social action, but I have not addressed the question: What is the task of the Church in the world today?

There was a time when the word 'mission' had a particular connotation. One thought of evangelistic campaigns, usually lasting about a week or a month, often taking place in the open air, in a tent or in a hall. The aim was quite simply to bring people to faith in Jesus Christ as their personal Saviour and Lord. There was also an eye to increasing church membership.

The word mission no longer has this narrow meaning and secular oganizations of all kinds now regularly refer to their 'mission statement'. Indeed that phrase is very much in vogue at the present time. It is in this sense of defining our primary aim that I am attempting now to discover what the role of the Church is to be in the purposes of God.

Firstly, a word of caution. It is not easy for any corporate body to produce a mission statement. The temptation is to state the obvious: 'the mission of this company of shoe manufacturers is to produce as many shoes as possible'. At first this seems without a doubt to be the primary aim. But is it? Suppose the market is already flooded with a surplus of cheap footwear from overseas. Simply producing more and more shoes would achieve only bankruptcy. Even qualifying the aim by adding the phrase 'the best quality shoes' might not help because it may be that at this time of recession particularly there might not be enough people willing to pay for the best shoes. The primary aim might have to refer to making profit.

I do not think the mission of the Church in the world is all that obvious. The purpose of the writer of the fourth Gospel is clearly stated: 'In order that you may hold the faith (or come to believe) that Jesus is the Christ, the Son of God, and that through this faith you may possess life by his name' (John 20:31). That surely is the aim of every preacher of the gospel, or at least it ought to be. But is this the mission statement of the Church as it confronts the world? I am not sure that it is.

In the beginning, God created the universe. The word creation has as part of its root meaning, 'to let be'. God is creative in the fullest possible meaning of the word and this implies originality. The writer of the first chapter of Genesis declares that God is pleased with everything he made. The children's hymn puts it:

> All things bright and beautiful,
> All creatures great and small,
> All things wise and wonderful,
> The Lord God made them all.

This reflection upon God's creative activity shows that one of the most important truths about life is that people, and perhaps things in some important respects, must be free to be themselves. History shows how hard it is for this truth to be fully acknowledged. Regrettably, the Church has not always acknowledged this truth. One immediately thinks of the Spanish Inquisition. But the situation in Northern Ireland is a more relevant example of how attitudes have hardened to the point of sectarian violence.

It is clear that if some Christian fundamentalist groups in the USA were able to seize power they would impose their own will in important areas of public life such as education, the media, legislation and health services. The whole atmosphere would become repressive. People living in any part of the world where there has been an Islamic fundamentalist revolution can testify to the climate of repression which those who do not share the revolutionary zeal experience. We must accept that unqualified democracy poses this threat to all minorities, but it is a fundamental tenet of Christian faith that the rights of minorities should be protected. It is a matter of pride for Baptists that it was one of their founders, Thomas Helwys, who wrote the first plea to the King of England for religious toleration. His words are remarkable for their fearless courage, bearing in mind that Helwys must have known the likely reaction of King James I to this challenge. Helwys wrote:

> Hear, O King, and despise not the counsel of the poor, and let their complaints come before thee. The King is a mortal man and not God: therefore hath no power over the immortal souls of his subjects, to make laws and ordinances for them, and set spiritual Lords over them. If the King have authority to make spiritual Lords and laws, then he is an immortal God, and not a mortal man. O King, be not seduced by deceivers to sin against God whom thou oughtest to obey, nor against thy subjects who ought and will obey thee in all things, with body, life and goods, or else let their lives be taken from the earth. God save the King.

Clearly the authorities could not ignore this challenge and Helwys was thrown into prison. It is believed he died there.

Taking seriously this concept of plurality, which seems to be inherent in the very creative activity of God and in an important Christian insight, we shall want to describe the mission of the Church not in any exclusive way, but on the contrary in a way which includes the great variety of people in the creative purposes of God.

Jesus went about doing good, even healing lepers who

121

were not grateful let alone believers, and proclaiming the kingdom of God. It is this kingdom of God, this 'rule of God', which is to be the centre of our attention and the goal of our endeavours. The Church is to be one of the main agents for bringing in the kingdom of God, but not to be equated with the kingdom of God.

This is how John Macquarrie describes the kingdom of God:

It would be a commonwealth of free beings, united in Being and with each other through love, yet since this is the love that lets-be, preserving a diversity that heightens the value of the unity far above that of any undifferentiated unity. (*Principles of Christian Theology*, p. 329)

Clearly, the kingdom of God has nowhere yet been fully realized, but all of us have had some experience which anticipates the kingdom of God. It is like when a group of people enjoy a really stimulating conversation when the topic is shared and everyone contributes some insight. These rare occasions are intimate, exciting and altogether wonderful. They are moments in time which belong to eternity. Indeed, we often forget time and are surprised at the lateness of the hour when we have to go our separate ways. This group experience is like a moment in the kingdom of God. The Last Supper was like that. It was like that when in the First World War one Christmas time, British and German soldiers came out of their trenches and played a game of football in no-man's-land.

The truth we must grasp is that the kingdom of God cannot be realized until everyone is included. The kingdom of God will be realized when love has broken down every barrier, when every wound has been healed and when every hurt has been turned to joy through reconciliation.

A great deal of what Jesus meant by the kingdom of God, and much of what the people listening to him would understand by the phrase, is contained in the Old Testament. The books of Moses described this desirable environment for living as a land flowing with milk and honey. It sounds a bit messy if we interpret the phrase too literally but we all understand this poetic image. The history of the kings of Israel seems to be a story mainly to do with a quest for territory but upon closer examination there is a remarkable account of the development of social organization and an impressive programme of domestic, religious and civic building.

The Psalms often complain that the moral and spiritual life of the community is not such as always to favour good living; there are violent people and those who live only for wrongly acquired wealth and are void of integrity. It all sounds rather familiar.

The Book of Proverbs deals with much of the nitty-gritty of day-to-day living.

The Hebrew prophets demand true spirituality and social justice.

All this Old Testament literature is the background to Jesus' work to promote the kingdom of God. It is an all-embracing view of life and is directed towards providing the conditions for all people to develop their full potential. This is far more exciting than simply making converts.

It is important that we continue to read the Old Testament and to be inspired by this revelation of God. We should remember the Old Testament was the Bible Jesus knew and often referred to in his preaching. The Old

Testament was the inspired Scriptures for the first generation of Christians before the Gospels were written. It is natural for us to give priority to the Gospels and for us to study the epistles to discover the elements of Christian theology, but we need to be aware that the New Testament does not contain the whole revelation of God. It has been a great disservice to the Church that the impression has sometimes been given that the New Testament supersedes the Old Testament. It does not. It confirms the Old Testament and takes the revelation of God a stage further. Of course, there are points where Jesus contradicts an item of Old Testament teaching, but that happens even within the books of the Old Testament. St Paul, it should be remembered, did a U-turn on circumcision (compare Acts 16:3 with Galatians 2:3–5).

The revelation of God is progressive and the Holy Spirit is still guiding the Church into truth. That is recognized by the concept of 'tradition' in the Roman Catholic Church and it is well expressed in the Protestant hymn:

> We limit not the truth of God
> To our poor reach of mind,
> By notions of our day and sect,
> Crude, partial, and confined;
> No, let a new and better hope
> Within our hearts be stirred:
> The Lord hath yet more light and truth
> To break forth from his word.

It is a great error for us to think that the Old Testament deals with the mere externals of religion and that the New Testament deals with the real questions of our standing before God. An erroneous view of the Old Testament, nowhere endorsed by our Lord, has led to a lopsided understanding of the kingdom of God. Let us state clearly: the kingdom of God will not be realized until the whole vision of life upon earth given in the Old and New Testaments of the Bible are fulfilled. We do not mean the coming true of some obscure passages of the Old Testament which some interpret as prophecies. We mean the achievement of conditions of life, both material and spiritual, which will ensure everyone having the chance to perfect their being. We doubt this will be achieved in time, but it is the goal we strive towards. And this should be the mission statement of the Church.

We must now turn to the matter of the means by which our mission is to be accomplished. A temptation for the Church is to accept the vision of the kingdom of God contained in the Bible and still being unfolded by the work of the Holy Spirit, but to say that the means of accomplishing this will be by leading every person to faith in our Lord Jesus Christ. There was a time when people did entertain the idea that it would be possible to convert every person of every language and nation to Christian faith. We can no longer contemplate this absurd idea. Experience teaches that even in those communities where there is an exceptionally high proportion of believers, the structures of society have not been transformed and people do not enjoy a proper freedom of expression.

One way of setting about the task of achieving the kingdom of God on earth is for every believer to do his or her best to apply the gospel to every part of their daily life. This is the approach recommended in passages of the New Testament such as the last two chapters of Ephesians. Believers are urged in the Lord's name to 'give up living like pagans with their good-for-nothing notions'.

The writer of the epistle refers to features of social life in his time which he particularly deplores: concupiscence, dishonesty, anger leading to violence, crime, vulgarity, fornication, indecency, greed and drunkenness. Christians are to give up all such vices. In addition to this transformation of personal character, believers are told to give particular attention to their domestic and working relationships.

It is in these matters of domestic and working relationships that present-day readers of the epistle are most critical. We can agree that by comparison with the standards of his day St Paul, or whoever is the writer, is quite liberated, but his acceptance of the subordination of women and the system of slavery is unacceptable today. We have made some progress although there is a long way to go. The important thing is that this epistle shows that it was understood from earliest times that the Christian gospel does not just apply to personal character and to family life, but also to matters such as industrial relations. Clearly, in today's society we shall want to take this out-working Christian faith much further.

The situation of Christians living in the first century after Christ is quite different from ours. In those days martyrdom was a real possibility and there was no opportunity for Christians to participate in any meaningful way in politics. Today we have a form of democracy which was achieved in no small measure by Puritans such as Oliver Cromwell, whose statue stands outside our Houses of Parliament, and by other notable dissenters. We must take much more seriously our Christian duty to participate in political debate and activity in order to take the transformation of society further on towards realizing our vision of the kingdom of God.

There can be no doubt about the importance of each individual doing what they can to put into practice their Christian faith in personal and civic life. But the days of the social entrepreneur are numbered. Individual effort, however strenuous and highly motivated, is no match for the corporate institutes which wield so much power. The notion is still alive in Britain that wealth is created by entrepreneurs, but other nations such as the Japanese have grasped the fact that in these days leadership is important but that investment in advanced technology and a well-organized work force are the real secrets of success. The church must also learn that individual witness is not enough. We must take more seriously the structures which are developing to enable us to work together across denominational boundaries. The partnership between the Anglican Bishop and Catholic Archbishop of Liverpool is a good example. Moreover, we must see much more investment by individual churches in ecumenical efforts to tackle urgent social problems at home and abroad.

It will be deplorable if for reasons of spiritual pride evangelicals withhold their support from such ecumenical endeavours.

Having given some thought to the task confronting the Churches, we are in a better position to draw up a spiritual profile of the kind of Christians we need to accomplish this.

We have thought about the creativity of God and accepted the necessity of plurality. We need to see people with different lifestyles, cultures and beliefs as varieties of being which God has permitted. What God has permitted, let us not refuse to acknowledge. Jesus admonished us to call no one a fool, because he saluted the divine in every person. To dismiss other people as worthless is to insult the image of God in them. One of the main features in our profile of Christian spirituality is that of genuine tolerance, far deeper than the tolerance of people with liberal opinions.

A second feature of our spiritual profile is the necessity of education. We are not here referring to mere academic discipline, although this is welcome. We are referring to a process of lifelong examination of one's beliefs and actions. We cannot admire religious naivety and theological ignorance.

I do not approve of any entrance test for church membership which a catechism or enquiries made by church visitors might suggest. The Church should be like a kind of Open University with no entrance requirements but a simple profession of faith in our Lord Jesus Christ and declaration of intent to try to follow his way. It should be understood that Christian discipleship requires constant mental activity and readiness for change. If we are to fulfil a world-transforming mission we must not let the emotional expression of faith take precedence over a coherent understanding of faith.

Without attempting to write a complete spiritual profile, I propose one more quality: faithfulness. There will be many reverses in the mission of the Church. There will be many reasons to doubt if the mission is capable of success. This is why we need Christians to be people who believe in God and will act in that faith right up to the end. That is the example of our Lord and of the Apostles and martyrs who have gone before us.

Who would true valour see,
Let him come hither;

Let Be

One here will constant be,
Come wind, come weather.
There's no discouragement
Shall make him once relent
His first avowed intent
To be a pilgrim.

(John Bunyan)

Reading List

Bax, J., *Meeting God Today* (DLT, 1990)

Bunyan, J., *Grace Abounding to the Chief of Sinners*

Bunyan, J., *Pilgrim's Progress*

Dix, G., *The Shape of the Liturgy* (A. & C. Black, 1945)

Fox, M., *Original Blessing* (Bear & Co., 1990)

Fox, M., *Western Spirituality* (Bear & Co., 1987)

Hill, C., *A Turbulent, Seditious and Factious People* (OUP, 1989)

Leech, K., *Spirituality and Pastoral Care* (Sheldon Press, 1986)

Macquarrie, J., *Paths in Spirituality* (SCM, 1972)

Macquarrie, J., *Principles of Christian Theology* (SCM, 1979)

Rauschenbusch, W., *A Theology of the Social Gospel*

Rauschenbusch, W., *Christianity and the Social Crisis*

Robinson, J., *Honest to God* (SCM, 1963)

Robinson, J., *Liturgy Coming to Life* (OUP, 1963)

Tillich, P., *The Protestant Era* (Nisbet, 1966)

World Council of Churches, *Ecumenical Perspectives on Baptism, Eucharist and Ministry*, ed. M. Thurian